PRAISE FOR
Then and Now

"*Then and Now* is narrated with the same homey bonhomie that has informed Ms. Cook's stage patter in recent years."

—*New York Times*

"Theater rats will savor Ms. Cook's account of her *Candide* audition in front of the show's composer, Leonard Bernstein. . . . It's clear in every word she sings that her wisdom is deep and hard-won."

—*Wall Street Journal*

"It's all here in Cook's memoir. Great theater, great people, not so great people, alcoholism, compulsive eating, an affair with actor Arthur Hill when they were both married to other people; the great love of the lady's life. A second career in cabaret that continues into her ninth decade."

—WOSU/NPR *New and Classical Music*

"And what a story it is, told in a bright, refreshing, and brutally honest voice, in a manner that you would expect from Barbara Cook. . . . Get yourself a copy of *Then and Now* and plunge into it, giving yourself breaks here and there to listen to Barbara sing."

—*Huffington Post*

"However grim the backstory—poverty, depression, alcoholism—the tone is still buoyant and down-to-earth."

—*New York* magazine

"Lively and frank."

—*Newsday*

"[A] piercingly candid, remarkably clear-eyed, hard-headedly optimistic narrative of a life well lived."

—*Everything Sondheim*

"Her talent has always been unique and her artistry superb. But this book is more a testament to Barbara's courage, strength, and determination to endure. The power of her inner voice, it turns out, matches the great gift of her outer one. How lucky we are to have now seen and heard both."   —Frank Langella

"I'm crazy about this book! Of course I've always been crazy about Barbara Cook. But who knew she had such a page-turner of a life? No wonder she makes us feel so deeply when she sings. It's a triumphant story of one of the greatest talents we've ever had. Bravo!"   —Barry Manilow

"I had the honor to share the stage eight shows a week with the legendary Barbara Cook. *Then and Now* is a must-read for all Broadway hopefuls. Her life lessons inspire, entertain, and demonstrate the guts needed to survive in show business."

—Vanessa Williams

Then and Now

THEN AND NOW

A MEMOIR

Barbara Cook

with Tom Santopietro

HARPER

NEW YORK · LONDON · TORONTO · SYDNEY

A hardcover edition of this book was published in 2016 by
HarperCollins Publishers.

THEN AND NOW. Copyright © 2016 by Barbara Cook. All rights
reserved. Printed in the United States of America. No part of this
book may be used or reproduced in any manner whatsoever without
written permission except in the case of brief quotations embodied in
critical articles and reviews. For information, address HarperCollins
Publishers, 195 Broadway, New York, NY 10007.

HarperCollins books may be purchased for educational, business,
or sales promotional use. For information, please email the Special
Markets Department at SPsales@harpercollins.com.

"Dancing in the Dark" (from *The Band Wagon*). Lyrics by Howard
Dietz, music by Arthur Schwartz © 1931 (renewed) WB Music
Corp. and Arthur Schwartz Music Ltd. All rights reserved. Used by
permission of Alfred Music.

FIRST HARPER PAPERBACK EDITION PUBLISHED 2017.

Designed by Fritz Metsch

Unless otherwise credited, all photographs are courtesy of the author.

Library of Congress Cataloging-in-Publication Data has been
applied for.

ISBN 978-0-06-209047-8 (pbk.)

17 18 19 20 21   LSC   10 9 8 7 6 5 4 3 2 1

For Adam

CONTENTS

PREFACE

SOMETIMES I WISH we were all cell phones. Yes, phones. The new mobile phones that exchange information with one click. Then I wouldn't have to write this whole book. It's not the time and the work involved, it's the talking about the hard stuff. I believe I'm an optimistic, positive person, but, you know, it's the painful stuff that really sticks out. I have had so many amazingly beautiful things happen in my life, but I think perhaps it's the difficulties and the bone-crunching crappy things that have really shaped who I am. I wonder who I would be if my little sister hadn't died when we were both so young. Oh, and how many times have I wondered who I would be if my father hadn't left when I was six years old.

I have been asked several times through the years to write my story. Frankly, most of the time I thought, "Who the hell cares?" But now I do feel that this book might help some people through bad times, might help them see that they can come out the other side and have a new life. F. Scott Fitzgerald wrote: "There are no second acts in American lives." Well, he was wrong. That's exactly what happened to me.

I did a lot of good work in the theater. God, how I loved it.

And then I became a drunk. I was depressed, and unemployable.

My life fell apart in lots of ways.

My son chose to live with his father instead of me. At the time

I thought that might kill me, but of course he made the right decision.

Then Wally Harper came along and helped me work again. What a coming-together that was. I stopped drinking a couple of years after we met. He was my accompanist, arranger, and friend for the next thirty years, and while I hated it when people said I had begun a second career, that's exactly what it was.

So here it is—the parts I can talk about. I don't want to hurt anybody. Of course a lot of people in my story are dead and can't be hurt anymore. I'm eighty-eight now, and that's one of the things that goes with age, isn't it—all kinds of loss.

But let me also tell you some of the great things about this business I've been in practically all my life. Because I never thought little Barbara Cook, sitting there dreaming on Ponce de Leon Avenue in Atlanta, would have anything resembling the life I've led—and, by God, I'm still having it.

Then and Now

I · CHILDHOOD

I KILLED MY sister when I was three years old. I was responsible for my father leaving us when I was six. I truly believed I was responsible for those events because my mother told me so. Now, that's not exactly what happened. You'll see what I mean later on. I had a lot to deal with before I became the person I am. We all have a lot to deal with. This is my story.

I was born; I breathed; I sang. I have no memory of a time when I didn't sing. No one in my family was a musician or singer, but my dad loved listening to music. He particularly loved Bing Crosby, while my granddaddy, Charlie Harwell, my mother's father, had a great love of music and theater. I didn't see him nearly as often as I would have liked because he and my grandmother, Minnie, were divorced, but he often came over to her house for the big Sunday supper she always cooked. On those occasions he would always ask me to sit on his knee and sing to him. He smelled of tobacco and whiskey, but I loved the way he smelled because I loved him. His scraggly old dog, Rags, would sit nearby, Granddaddy's battered fedora on his head and his pipe in his mouth, while I would sing "Indian Love Call" to Granddaddy. Dear sweet Charlie Harwell. He was a darling man.

God, how I loved to sing and prance around and dream and pretend. Somewhere around 1932, when I was five years old, my mother and dad took me to see my first stage show. I was in heaven.

When we came home I whooped around the room, singing and dancing all the parts for them. They were delighted, and I remember loving the fact that they were enjoying me.

My daddy was a traveling salesman whose specialty was ladies' millinery. Everybody wore hats in those days; a lady or a gentleman just didn't go out without a hat, and ladies would complete the picture by always wearing gloves. Daddy would usually call home two or three times during the week when he was on the road, and he always asked me to sing for him over the phone. He mostly traveled to neighboring states, but sometimes he went as far as Texas, and then he would bring back Texas boots for me. I loved them. I don't remember other little girls having boots, but they fit right into my tomboy life.

As I write this I realize that my happy childhood memories almost invariably revolve around my daddy. I adored him because we had so much fun together. Every morning when he was home he would turn on the radio so that we could listen to *Don McNeill's Breakfast Club*. Every day McNeill would ask us to "march around the breakfast table," so Daddy and I would stoutly march around the table, singing and laughing. He was my protector and my defender. When, for some reason, at the age of five or six, my mother wanted me to eat baby food, right out of the jar, I violently objected. It was strained spinach, a truly hideous taste, and I was *six*, not one. My mother insisted: "Eat that spinach!" My dad said: "Let me taste it." Then—"God, Nell, how can you ask her to eat this stuff?" End of debate.

My father was thrilled to be a parent. My mother later told me that he would cry every month when once again she had not become pregnant, and when I was conceived he was ecstatic. He always made me feel loved, but the truth is that he really wanted a son. I must have somehow understood that, and was delighted at Christmastime when I was five years old and got an Indian suit, a cowboy suit, a drum, and a tool chest. Together Daddy and I cut an airplane out with my new saw from the tool chest and had great fun putting the pieces together. I loved playing cowboys and Indians and beating my little drum. I also received a doll that year. I named her Buttercup, and then proceeded to totally forget about her. There's no question but that some aspects of that persona persist in me to this day. I was recently talking to my friend Sybil and she was chattering happily about how much she enjoys having her nails done every week. That's just the sort of activity that holds absolutely no interest for me. I really am an eighty-eight-year-old tomboy!

My father supplied the fun in our household, but my mother could be a very difficult personality. For instance: one Easter my parents gave me a sweet little yellow chick that I adored. I'd lie on the floor and it would hop all over me. Of course little chicks become big chicks, and one day when I couldn't find my little pet, my mother told me it had scurried onto our back terrace and fallen down three stories to the yard, where the rats ate it. I found out years later that of course that's not what happened at all. Clearly they had to get rid of this growing chicken, and they gave my chick to friends who had a farm outside of Atlanta. Why my mother didn't just explain that to me in the beginning puzzled me for ages, but I finally came to the conclusion that she couldn't bear to take the blame for having taken my pet away. Somehow she felt it was better to lie to me and make up a dreadful story about rats eating her than risk my anger about the chick's permanent vacation in the country. Sometimes my mother meant well, sometimes she didn't, but often her reasoning remained unfathomable.

I want to be fair to my mother, yet it's difficult to talk about her and be fair, because she'll never be able to give her side of the story. My mother was two people, and I never knew which mother I was going to get, the good or the bad. She could be very funny, and she could be outrageously generous with me, but that's not how I remember her for the most part. So much of what she said and did injured me. I believe she loved me. I know she did. But her idea of love was a complete incorporation of my life into hers. I think she had no concept of my being a person separate from her. No boundaries existed. None whatsoever.

The truth is, to my now adult eyes my parents seem like a pair of mismatched opposites. My father, Charles Bunyan Cook, was born in 1900, a native Georgian just like my mother, Nellie Mae Harwell, who was one year younger. They met in a neighborhood ice cream parlor—he was a salesman and she worked as a switchboard operator for Southern Bell. They must have loved each other, but they were vastly different people. My dad loved music and language, books and ideas. He introduced me to the novels of Thomas Wolfe, loved teaching me new words, and gave me my enduring love of crossword puzzles. My mother, sadly, shared little of this. I remember having only what I call "meat-and-potatoes" conversations with my mother. We never talked about ideas.

They could not have been more different, but at the very start of their courtship something clearly clicked. One day, after my mother died, I found some old correspondence between them, all written on very old-fashioned notes and cards, covered in chiffon flowers topped with shiny glitter. In the cards I found beautiful vows of undying love. When my dad was in the cavalry, stationed in Seattle during the First World War, long-distance phone calls to his sweetheart Nellie were out of the question, so in order to feel closer to each other they agreed to both go outside and look at the moon at the same time. One in Seattle, one in Atlanta. Romantic. Touching.

I tell myself—and I believe—that it all started well for them; and when I was born, on October 25, 1927, it seems like life was fairly solid for them. My younger sister, Molly Patricia, was born eighteen months after me, and my memories of that time are very happy ones.

My sister was so pretty; she had big, round, brown eyes and lovely light-brown, softly curling hair. My blond hair was straight as a stick, and oh how I envied her curls. I have a photograph taken in the backyard of our house on Oak Street, and Pat's beautiful curls are certainly in evidence, but as she comes down the back steps she looks thin and frail, with dark circles under her sweet eyes.

She must have died shortly after the photograph was taken because she was only eighteen months old when she passed away. Pat had recovered from pneumonia some time before her death; I was three at the time, and my mother told me that the doctor said Pat's lungs had been severely weakened and if she ever contracted pneumonia again it could be very serious. Soon she was suffering from double pneumonia, a dangerous disease for anyone in the early 1930s, but particularly so for a baby. This was before antibiotics, and treatment was rudimentary at best.

To make things even more difficult, I had caught whooping cough right before Pat contracted double pneumonia. I had recovered, but not before passing it on to Pat. She was not in a hospital, I believe, because they felt there was nothing they could do to help her. My mother's child was dying, and she felt helpless: "What can I do for her? Does she need the window open more? Or closed? Should I cover her? Dear God, what can I do to help her?"

Increasing my mother's desperation was the knowledge that at the exact same time, her big brother, Ralph, was fighting for his life after having been shot just a few days earlier. He had been sitting in a police car with a friend who was on the force when a man just released from prison came looking for vengeance and shot my uncle, having missed his intended victim, the uniformed policeman. My mother went to the cemetery to bury her brother, whom she adored, and the very next day returned to bury her daughter. She must have been crazed with grief.

Since I was only three, it was decided that I was too young to go to Pat's funeral. But I have a very clear memory of my father lifting me up in his arms, carrying me to the kitchen window, and painting a smiling face on the palm of my hand with Mercurochrome: "While we're gone, open your hand and look at this little face. That will cheer you up until we come back." Daddy was burying his daughter, too, but somehow he was able to think of me that morning, trying his very best to cheer me up. I loved him very much.

I don't remember crying over my sister's death, and I don't remember my own feelings with all this chaos swirling around me. Even at three, however, I knew that something was very wrong, and when family and friends got back to the house after the funeral I found a way to communicate that all was not right with me. People were lined up across the front porch on this very hot July day, rocking back and forth and fanning themselves, when I had what I thought was a great idea. I picked up the garden hose lying in the front yard and turned it on full force, dousing everybody in sight. My uncle Johnny, my dad's brother, rushed out to stop me, but not before he got completely soaked.

We moved after my sister's death. Our new home was a small

ground-floor, one-room apartment with a little attached kitchen. We must have lived there for several years, because when I look at photographs from that time I can see how much I changed physically from year to year—but the background in those photos remained the same. Our lives, of course, were filled with sadness after my sister's death, but there were still aspects of our new home that I liked, most notably a nice big backyard with a swing. I have a picture of me in that swing with a playmate. She's a pretty little girl with long, Shirley Temple curls, neatly dressed, with her shoes and socks looking perfect. I'm sitting next to her, with not much on—just a little pair of panties, legs all spread out, no shoes or socks, Dutch Boy haircut. There is nothing girly about me at all. I look like a miniature W. C. Fields—all I need is a straw hat and cigar.

The truth is, it didn't matter that much to me where we lived. We were just trying to regain some semblance of "normal life," and when, after a year or two in that ground-floor studio, we moved again, to a one-bedroom apartment with a little banistered porch off the living room, the change didn't really affect me.

My sister's death would have left a dark and lasting impression on my life under any circumstances, but for me the loss was compounded by a brutal sense of guilt. Sadly, I believe that guilt was instilled in me by my mother. For years I had a powerful memory of my mother standing before me, saying, "If you hadn't given Pat whooping cough, she would have lived." I grew up believing I was responsible for my sister's death. That's what I took in, and what I lived with for many years. I would casually say, "I gave my sister whooping cough" and believe it was the truth, because somehow my mother had made me feel it was.

I see it differently now, but no matter how much I understand, intellectually, that I had nothing to do with Pat's death, somewhere in my unconscious lies the residue of the belief that I killed my sister. My first therapist wisely asked me the question, "Has it ever occurred to you that you didn't give her whooping cough? That she caught it?" Now, after a lot of work, I believe that memories can lie, and on that dreadful day when my mother, mad with grief, had to go back to the cemetery for the second day in a row, she, within my hearing, may have said to someone, "If only Barbara hadn't given Pat whooping cough, she might have lived."

As my friend Stephen Sondheim wrote in one of his typically wise and double-edged lyrics: "Children will listen."

The result of all this is that I have often felt I didn't deserve all the good things coming to me. Now I've come to believe that we gain only the success we believe we deserve.

WE SOON MOVED again, this time into a third-floor apartment on Memorial Drive. It was a very nice apartment but just one bedroom, so I suppose we all slept in one room. This was the continuation of lots of moving around for me; and until I found my present apartment, in 1976, I never lived in any one location for more than five years.

It seems my parents' marriage never really recovered from Pat's death, and next to my sister's death, the most indelible memory of my childhood is that of my father leaving us three years later. He is standing at the door of our apartment on Memorial Drive, and he turns back just before he leaves. My mother is hysterical. A jagged, flailing lump of hysteria. I'm on the couch, kicking and screaming, "Daddy, Daddy, don't go, don't go." I don't remember anything he says as he walks off. The door shuts behind him and my life is changed forever.

For some reason I never completely understood, my first therapist said he didn't believe the scene as I remember it. Some years ago, however, I was undergoing hypnotherapy, which I have found to be very helpful. I dutifully counted back from ten, and as usual I was not feeling hypnotized but thought I was just "going along with things." All of a sudden I saw myself walking down a brick sidewalk with a picket fence on my right. I blurted out: "I'm a man." Then: "I'm my father." I was shocked. This had never happened before. Suddenly I was my father standing in the doorway, looking back at the scene I've described above. I saw the entire event from his point of view and understood deeply that he had to leave. I felt his pain at leaving me but I knew he had no other choice. His intention was not to leave me. He had to break away from my mother.

It was quite a breakthrough, but the issue of abandonment remains. Decades later, when I would go out with my musical director/accompanist Wally Harper to see a concert or play, I'd want to talk about it after the show, but he would have already planned to take off to attend some late party. Wally's leaving to attend a party was very hard for me to take. I really believe it's because of the childhood abandonment issues. Six decades had passed, but the feeling remained.

My father had walked out, my mother had already told me that I had, in effect, killed my sister, and when, on the same afternoon that he left I wanted to go out to play, my mother held my shoulders and looked at me sternly. *Under no circumstances*, she said, *was I to tell anyone what had happened*. There was still a sense of shame about a broken marriage, and at age six I felt ashamed.

Just to add to the weight of events, my father had recently been in the hospital for a minor hernia operation, and my mother told me that he'd had an affair with one of the nurses taking care of him. An affair right after abdominal surgery? True? Who the hell knows! Appropriate information for a six-year-old? Hardly! And why would anyone convey all that to a very young child in the first place? Later on the night my father left, my mother brought me into her bed. And that never changed. I slept in bed with my mother every night until I was twenty years old and decided to make New York my home.

When my father left, my mother laid another burden of guilt upon me. She said, "If Pat had lived, your father would not have left." So, according to my mother, Pat could have kept my father with us; I was responsible for Pat's death; so I had screwed *that* up as well. After Daddy left, whenever I was going to see him, my mother told me I should beg him to come back to us. If I did it right, she said, I could convince him to come back. Of course he never came back, and I always felt that I had failed miserably again. If I had to give a color to my life during the years before my daddy left, it would all be a golden sunny yellow. After he walked out it changed to a heavy, dull gray.

Although I would see my father often in the years ahead, I didn't see him in ways that were satisfying. He had remarried and moved to North Carolina for work. My time with him was always short and felt stolen, on the run, while he was in town.

My father couldn't afford to keep my mother and me in our present apartment, so she decided we would move in with her mother until she could figure out what to do. The truth is that my mother was so devastated from losing my father that she probably was not functioning well enough to make any decisions about how to go on with her life. My father was not coming back, and we were now going to live in a cheerless house at 366 Glenwood Avenue with my grandmother Harwell and three of my mother's sisters. Very shortly after we moved in, my mother became ill with pneumonia and I remember living with the fear that I would lose her, just as I had lost the rest of my family.

The apartment we were living in when my father left was very comfortable. We had electricity, heat, hot running water, and a comfortable bathroom. When we moved in with my grandmother, we had none of those things. Suddenly I was living with kerosene lamps and ineffectual fireplaces for warmth. If we wanted hot water, it had to be heated on the iron stove in the kitchen. The house was wired, but we couldn't afford to pay for electricity. This was during the Depression, right in the city of Atlanta.

My grandmother's house on Glenwood was a two-family gray wood house. Gray in color, gray in atmosphere. My God, what a change for me. With the exception of my mother's two younger twin sisters, Doris and Dorothy, there was not a lot of love and kindness going on. Five women and me, all living in two rooms without electricity or heat.

My grandmother was a hard woman. Actually, she and my mother were somewhat alike, a fact that certainly helps explain why there was often tension between them. God knows, my grandmother had a hell of a life. She was divorced from my granddaddy, Charlie, and in the 1920s that did not make for an easy state of affairs. She could be ornery and divisive, and as a result there was constant chaos in her house.

My handicapped aunt Dorothy, my grandmother, my mother, and I all slept in two beds in the middle room, the feather beds smelling of urine and God knows what else. My aunts Doris and Margaret slept on cots in the front room—the living room—and in the third, back, room was the kitchen with a kerosene stove along one wall and a black iron woodstove against another. A big round oak table was in the center of the room. Through the kitchen was the door to the back porch, where the icebox lived.

Although a bathroom had been added to my grandmother's back porch (a big improvement, because they had been living with only an outhouse in the backyard), there was no heat or hot water in the bathroom, and tub baths during the winter proved impossible. Instead, we all washed in the kitchen, dabbing soap and water on ourselves from a big gray pan of water that had been heated on the woodstove. Even in the warmer months a bath could turn into a big project because all the water had to be heated in dishpans and carried out to the porch, pan by pan.

I suppose there were electric heaters of some sort in those years, but even though the wires were in evidence, the electricity had been cut off long ago. It was the Depression, and there was simply no money to pay for electricity. I could deal with the heat in the summertime, but it was cold in the winter, and without heat or electricity the cold stayed in your bones. All six of us were just plain uncomfortable.

We had kerosene lamps and small fireplaces in the two front rooms, and I did my homework by the light of those kerosene lamps. I was not a particularly good student for a simple reason: if the subject didn't interest me, then I put no effort into it. In my high school years I earned very good grades but failed geometry because I had no interest in it and couldn't see how it could be of any possible use to me. Honestly, I still don't.

My mother's sisters were quite a trio. Margaret was most always angry and didn't have much to do with me, except to snarl at me from time to time. She had hennaed red hair, very curly, and even with that sour disposition she had a sweet boyfriend who was tall and so thin that everyone of course called him "Fats." Fats and Margaret were going to be married after the war, but he never came back and she married Horace Poss instead. Her taste was typical of the world I knew in my grandmother's house. She collected salt and pepper shakers, and I remember very well her favorites: two little boys sitting on chamber pots labeled "Billy Can" and "Billy Can't." Lord, help us!

I adored my aunt Doris, who was blond, beautiful, and, to my seven-year-old self, perfect. Only twelve years older than I, she taught me to draw, and from her I learned the words to the songs she loved: "Winter Wonderland," "Bei Mir Bis Du Schoen"— all the hits of the 1930s and early forties. She taught me the latest dances—the Shag, the Big Apple, the Little Peach—and her kindness provided me a measure of comfort and security. I loved Doris, and it was sad to hear about her eventually sinking into alcoholism toward the end of her life. It's a stark fact that my mother was one of eight children, four of whom were ultimately alcoholic.

My aunt Dorothy, Doris's twin, was born with a curvature of the spine, and, according to my mother, it was the doctor's fault. Dorothy was sweet and fragile—but she was a sweet and fragile tyrant. She could sit up for a few hours in her big wooden rolling chair, but other than that she lay in bed all day, drooling and kicking and flailing uncontrollably. We played Old Maid and other little games and made designs with colorful, shiny little clay beads, and I loved her. When my school friends came to visit they were frightened of her, but I wasn't. I was used to her. She was a constant strange playmate, a frail tyrant who went crazy if my grandmother even hinted at leaving the house, which made my grandmother a prisoner in her own home. Finally my grandmother just never left the house at all, and it was no surprise when, after her mother died, Dorothy lived for only one more week. She couldn't exist without her mother.

A very sweet old couple, the Drums, lived in the other half of the house. I was terrified of their huge German shepherd dog, and in their kitchen they kept a mean, screechy cockatoo that scared the hell out of me every time I ventured within sight of its cage. Mrs. Drum tried to reassure me by telling me the bird thought I was a monkey and that's why he made that god-awful noise when I came near. She took great interest in me, and loved having me sing to her. It was a blessing to be able to visit with this sweet lady and get away from the other side of the house.

The Great Depression had hit, but so had my own six-years-old depression. Don't ever doubt that kids can be depressed. How could I not be? My sister had died. My father had left, even though I had cried and begged him not to go. My mother had been ill with pneumonia. I was scared. Always.

When my mother recovered from her pneumonia, she looked endlessly for work, any kind of work, walking into town in order to save the bus fare. Night after night she'd walk dejectedly back home, the job search having proved utterly futile. My aunts Doris and Margaret did have employment, however, working at the Standard Coffee Company, where their jobs consisted of bagging the beans, hour after numbing hour. Under their skirts they wore long bloomers that had elastic just above the knees, and some of that coffee found its way into their bloomers; other foodstuffs might have been in short supply, but we never lacked for coffee. It was great fun watching them pull the elastic away from their knees and seeing the coffee beans come tumbling out.

My mother was sad and depressed. In hindsight, I understand how fragile she must have felt, but in her loneliness she shared wildly inappropriate information with me. Our house was near Grant Park, with its big lake, and one night when I found her crying, she blurted out her plan to go to the park, walk into the lake, and drown herself. It was 1934 and I was seven years old.

Of course I developed all sorts of nervous fears. I thought that my mother was going to die, just like my sister. Atlanta has always had severe lightning storms during the summer, and when one of those storms came roaring through, I was petrified that my mother would be hit by lightning and instantly die. Storms terrified me, and I remember on one of those terrifying afternoons that Mrs. Drum comforted me by telling me that my mother would be safe from the lightning because the hat she was wearing included a rubber band that would protect her. But it all weighed on me, this constant fear of being lost and alone with no one to take care of me except my tough grandmother. My young life had fallen apart.

It was at this time that a fire-and-brimstone preacher set up a tent in a nearby vacant lot and for several weeks held an old-fashioned revival meeting. One hot summer evening my mother and some of her friends went to one of the meetings, and she took me with her. During the sermon the preacher said that if Jesus had come to us and we had refused him we would burn in hell for eternity. Make that ETERNITY. In my young mind I was thinking that perhaps Jesus had come to me and I hadn't realized it. I was sure I was doomed. That night began a pattern of my waking in the night, gasping for breath, filled with a dread certainty that I was dying right at that very moment. Now I recognize these episodes as panic attacks, but then I was seven years old, wetting the bed again, and waking up thinking I was dying.

The attacks and the bed-wetting continued, and my mother took me to the doctor. Nobody had connected my panic to the preacher's fire-and-brimstone sermon, but when the good doctor discovered that the first attack had happened hours after I had gone to the revival meeting, he simply said, "Don't take her to any more revival meetings." End of discussion.

Our house was in a constant state of chaos, but there was always food of some sort, and I never went to bed on an empty stomach. It's striking to realize how many of my childhood memories revolve around food: oatmeal with loads of sugar. Evaporated milk.

Peanut-butter-and-raisin sandwiches when I came home from school. Tea every morning with evaporated milk and so much sugar it remained a sludge in the bottom of the cup.

My daddy's mom was the best cook in the family, but we were living with my mama's mother, and she made what she called goulash—elbow macaroni with tomatoes and green peppers. There would be delicious home fries and dripping-with-grease apricot or peach turnovers made in the frying pan. Fried tripe. Salmon croquettes. It sounds sumptuous but it was basic and it had to feed six women. The big meal of the week, which they cooked on the kerosene stove, was Sunday dinner. I actually came to dread those Sunday-afternoon meals on account of the kerosene stove: the fumes from the kerosene were so awful that I couldn't go into the kitchen without my eyes streaming tears and my throat burning.

We were desperately poor. So often you hear people say, "We were poor but we didn't know it"—well, I knew it. I felt so deprived. One of my chores was fetching kerosene from the store in a can. The can had lost its cork, so my grandmother had a small sweet potato screwed into the top. I was deeply embarrassed to walk down the street carrying a can with a sweet potato sticking out of it, so I finally refused. The solution was to put the can in a paper bag, which soon got stained from the kerosene; in the end, the paper bag proved to be just as mortifying as the sweet potato.

MY ANXIETY PROBLEMS were not the only ailments I suffered from as a child. When I was about seven or eight it was discovered that I was anemic, but this turned out to be a really good thing. The doctor prescribed exercise, and I talked my mother into letting me have tap lessons. I took to it instantly, and earned the first money I ever made—fifty cents!—performing a little military tap number in between shows at a movie house. That money went a long way in the 1930s: fifty cents would buy ten loaves of bread or ten quarts of milk.

I especially adored movies, spending as much time in movie theaters as I could—the better to escape my unhappiness at home. The movies were a readily accessible, dream-fulfilling way to drift into a different, more glamorous, and altogether more wonderful world. It was actually from the movies that I learned to love classical music: Nelson Eddy and Jeanette MacDonald were my absolute idols. Lauritz Melchior and Kirsten Flagstad. Grace Moore. For a poor little girl in Georgia the very names evoked a world of culture and glamour. I had a bedroom with no windows which opened on to an inner stairwell, and I would sit on the floor, light candles, and listen to classical music for hours on end.

At a very early age my Saturday afternoons were given over to the Metropolitan Opera broadcasts. All the neighborhood kids would be out in the yard playing and I would be inside listening to the opera, utterly transported by the music. Here was grand opera from the biggest, brightest city of them all—New York. So swept away was I by the broadcasts that I didn't rush out to play with the kids after the program concluded. In fact, if I heard a performance that really impressed me, I couldn't bear for anybody to speak to me afterward. I wanted to remain inside that experience, become the story or the protagonist myself. I was not, to say the least, the easiest kid to be around.

When I was twelve years old the world premiere of *Gone With the Wind* was held in Atlanta. You can't imagine what that novel meant to Atlanta, and the movie was even more momentous. The city staged a parade for the film's premiere, and I remember standing on Peachtree Street with my mother that evening before scurrying to the Lowes Grand, which had been redecorated with a false façade to look like Tara. And finally, there they were— sitting in the back of their open cars—Clark Gable, Carole Lombard, Vivien Leigh, Laurence Olivier. WOW! Many years later I was at a party and met Vivien Leigh. I was performing in *She Loves Me* and she was in the process of winning a Tony Award for her performance in *Tovarich*, her one Broadway musical. My leading man, Daniel Massey, introduced us and of course I wanted to tell her how much that far-away evening in Atlanta had meant to me; when I broached the subject she all but froze and almost literally turned away from me. I think I'd stupidly told her how old I was that night in Atlanta and she sure as hell didn't want to hear about that.

Going to the movies consumed the little spending money I had. I would get twenty-five cents to spend on a Saturday: the movie cost ten cents, I'd get a hamburger for ten, and a dill pickle for five. That was my treat. The Temple was our local movie house, and I was sometimes in there longer than the ushers. I'd start with the first show in the morning and see the picture four times in a row. One of my aunts would eventually come storming down the aisle looking for me. I literally had to be dragged out of the theater.

What I loved most of all was any movie that had a stage show at the center of the plot: movies like *42nd Street* and all of the Mickey and Judy "let's put on a show" extravaganzas. And—at the very top of my list: Jeanette MacDonald and Nelson Eddy. As a youngster, the idea of being in films seemed outrageous to me—Jeanette seemed like an untouchable goddess—so I fixated on the idea of performing onstage. I remember saying that I wanted to perform in "musical comedy" even before I knew what musical comedy was.

I saw every one of Jeanette and Nelson's movies ten or twelve times. I just loved them—no, I wanted to *be* them. I wanted to be both of them. Here's how much my love for Jeanette impressed itself on my brain: at some point during the 1970s I began telling people, "The most wonderful thing has happened to me. Jim Broderick and I were having lunch at the Russian Tea Room. I looked across the way and there was Agnes de Mille. And guess who was sitting with her—Jeanette MacDonald! I said to Jim, 'Please excuse me. I have to table hop a second.' I went over and met JEANETTE MACDONALD!! 'Oh!'" I'd tell everyone. "'She was so nice and so beautiful.'" I told everyone this story. There was just one problem: it never happened.

Some years after this supposed meeting I was looking through the latest *Theatre World*, which is an annual publication about the most recent theater season. And in the front of the book were photographs of actors who had died. And oh my God—it turned out that Jeanette died before I even met Jim Broderick! WHAM!!

Something's wrong here. I talked to Jim Broderick about it. He said to me, "We never had lunch at the Russian Tea Room." I asked Agnes de Mille, who shot me a look and said, "I never met you at the Russian Tea Room." I wasn't lying and it wasn't a dream—I just completely and totally believed it. So—it looks like you can't trust anything I say . . .

The movies provided much-needed solace during my childhood, because my mother and I moved around a lot, having left my grandmother's after a particularly acrimonious "falling out" between my mother and grandmother. Actually I'm not sure they ever had a "falling in," so contentious was their relationship—two strong-willed women butting heads over issues both large and small. My mother found a job as a telephone operator at the Biltmore Hotel, and sometimes she couldn't avoid taking the night shift. I'd come home from school and in order to avoid being alone in our dark, solitary apartment, I would go to the corner drugstore and do my homework at the counter. The man there was very kind and would give me a soda, probably because he felt sorry for me. Eventually I'd have to go home. Oh, how fearful I was. We lived in one room in a big emptyish dark, dark building. I remember rushing up big, wide stairs before slamming the door shut. I'd bolt the door before drifting off into an uneasy sleep.

I spent a great deal of time on my own, yet in some ways I was hopelessly immature when it came to the requirements of daily living. My mother did everything for me, a state of affairs which, believe it or not, seemed to have begun with her visit to a fortune-teller when I was eight years old. This visit occurred during the Depression, when a lot of people visited fortune-tellers because of life's uncertainties. Off my mother went to the fortune-teller, and when she returned home a few hours later, she sat me down and with great portent relayed what the fortune-teller had told her. She took my hands in hers and, leaning close to me, explained that the fortune-teller said I was going to be a great singer—that unlike other children I was a creative artist and that she should never expect me to do any sort of menial work. She shouldn't ask me to wash dishes and do normal chores around the house—and she never again did. I was always free to dream and read and listen to the music that I loved. In other words, I grew completely out of touch with the ways of the world.

By the time I got to high school my mother had moved us to one of the nicer areas in Atlanta, called Druid Hills. We were actually just on the edge of Druid Hills, living in the worst apartment in a nice building. I went to school at Girls High School, one of only four high schools in all of Atlanta in those years. I didn't know a lot of people there who had the same interests I did, namely music, art, and theater. The other girls were interested in clothes, and I couldn't afford clothes. I got teased about wearing the same clothes all the time. They joined sororities, which I couldn't afford, and it was unusual to have divorced parents. I just did not fit in. I had one particularly close friend in high school, Jo Forrester, who was one year older and shared my passions, but for the most part I felt alienated from the rest of the kids, set apart both by my comparative poverty and by my interests.

And yet, I made momentous discoveries there, too. Although I had been tap dancing for years, as well as singing in Christmas pageants and in the school production of *The Pirates of Penzance*, it was during a high school English class that I was struck with the thought that I might have some acting talent, too. We were all doing scenes from plays, and for some reason I chose a solo scene from a play about an older married couple. The man is dying, but his wife has assured him he will live long enough to hear the cuckoo in the spring. She knows he won't really live that long, so she goes out in the garden and pretends to be the cuckoo. It sounds laughable to me now, and I can imagine it being greeted with titters by high school kids. But nobody laughed—in fact, everybody was in tears. I remember the teacher saying that in all the time she'd been teaching she'd never heard anything like it. I was good—I could act!

I was dying to tell my mother. But somehow I waited until we'd had dinner. Then I sat her down and said, "I have something very important to tell you. I can act." It was clear that it didn't mean a thing to her. "That's nice, dear," I think she said. In later years she took great pride in my performances, but at the time I think she couldn't fully believe that I had any talent. I was such an extension of her, and she had such a low opinion of herself, that she couldn't believe that I could be exceptional.

If it had been possible to open our skins and pull us together, that's what my mother would have done. She had no one else, so she poured all of her need for intimacy into me. We slept in the same bed all those years, not so much out of financial straits—although certainly we were always poor—but because of her need.

This unnatural idea—that I was part of her, that I *was* her—manifested itself in a far more sinister way on at least one occasion. My mother rarely dated, but one Saturday night when I was just ten or eleven she invited a man over for dinner. We were living in a one-room apartment with a Murphy bed, so I simply pulled the bed down and went to sleep when it was my bedtime. At one point I woke up, with the lights out in the room and my mother and this fellow necking on the sofa. I went back to sleep, and when I woke up the next morning, my leg thrown around what I assumed was my mother, I found that the body next to me was her date from the night before. He had apparently had too much to drink, and, unbelievably enough, she let him sleep in the bed with me, rather than on the sofa. She probably thought the man should get the most comfortable spot—the bed. Never mind the fact that she was putting this man in bed with her young daughter. Better that than making him sleep on the couch . . .

It was the first time I remember not just being mad at my mother but being volcanically enraged. She didn't seem to understand how violated I felt. I don't think she could grasp how appalling it was because once again she felt me to be such a part of her that it was as if it had been her sleeping in bed with him. Fortunately he was so drunk that there was no danger of something truly terrible happening. Sadly, I think my mother never understood what an egregious thing she had done.

GROWING UP IN Atlanta, I thought there was something wrong with me because I never felt that I fit in. I was like a little girl with her face pressed against the glass of life and I couldn't get in. I dreamed of New York—literally, and in color.

I had actually taken a brief school trip to Manhattan when I was still in the W. F. Slaton Grammar School. The principal was a very kind woman who realized I had some talent, and nurtured me: I had crooked teeth and perhaps with an eye toward my undertaking a performing career, she talked to me about fixing them, but of more immediate benefit to me at age twelve was the fact that she made my trip to New York possible. Students who worked as school crossing guards were rewarded with a trip to the 1939 World's Fair in New York, and although I was not one of them, the principal allowed me to go on the trip. We were required to pony up about ten dollars; now, my mother made thirteen dollars a week, so this was a huge sum for us, but she made sure I had it because she knew how much it meant to me. Here was a first step toward answering the refrain I was already hearing with increasing frequency from family friends, teachers, and even total strangers: "You should go to New York. You could sing in the theater."

First stop on the train was Washington, D.C., but I have no memory of that part of the journey. It was the New York City glimpsed in the movies that had always captured my imagination, and when we finally arrived in Manhattan, it was completely mind-blowing to be walking down the very streets I had seen onscreen. I had no idea that many of the movies I loved were shot on Hollywood studio sets—to me it was all the same. The New York of the movies equaled the New York I was now avidly exploring.

The World's Fair itself was the highlight, but I also had the chance to see my first Broadway show, *The Hot Mikado*, which was an all-black swing version of the Gilbert and Sullivan operetta, starring Bill "Bojangles" Robinson. The show seems, in retrospect, a curious choice for a bunch of Georgia kids. Maybe they reasoned that Gilbert and Sullivan would at least be good, clean fun? Believe it or not, I left at intermission. My first Broadway show, and I was somehow unimpressed.

I can't say I stepped off the train back in Atlanta fired with the knowledge that I would return to Manhattan and storm the city with my talent. But as I grew up and continued to perform, it naturally became the focus of my dreams. I kept tapping throughout my high school years, even as I began to discover the glimmerings of an acting gift. Just before entering high school I had joined the chorus line put together by a woman named Mrs. I. W. Curry. She organized performances for the Elks and Masons in various small towns in Georgia. Each of the girls in the tap line performed a specialty number, and there was often a guest star, usually a musician or a tumbler. This was before the USO existed, and we occasionally performed for servicemen at Fort Benning. I had a sweet, light soprano, and I remember resenting, just a little, that I never earned quite as much applause as Marguerite Davis, who really wowed the boys with her flirtatious version of "You Made Me Love You."

But the opportunities to perform in Atlanta were relatively few, even after I won an amateur singing contest at age fifteen singing

"My Devotion." The singing contest, oddly enough, was part of a rather polite burlesque show. When I told them I could tap, they offered me a job with the show. The law said I had to be sixteen but I was only fifteen, so of course I lied and became the newest member of the so-called Tiller Line (the concept of a line of girls kicking their legs up was first created by a man named Tiller). In show-biz lingo, the dancers were also called "ponies." I worked in the show all through the summer of 1943, and with the two young daughters of the producer in the show, there was nothing really down and dirty going on. At one point there were two semi-nudes onstage—one painted gold and the other painted silver. The law insisted they stay absolutely still. One move and we could all be carted off to the hoosegow. That was the first professional show I was ever a part of. It was hard work—several shows a day, and long hours—but I was earning money, and sometimes they allowed me to sing in the overture, which meant earning twenty-five dollars extra per week.

Because I was pretty short next to the showgirls, I was always a "pony." But—in the final shows, before I went back to high school, they let me be a showgirl. They gave me the highest heels they could find and stuffed my bra to the gunnels. I had a ball prancing around in all my feathers and sequins. The only negative was that working in a burlesque show—tepid or not—earned me a questionable reputation, and at least one mother refused to allow her daughter to double-date with me.

After graduating from high school I glumly fell into a series of routine clerical jobs for which I was singularly unqualified. The war had ended in August of 1945 and I went to work for the government as a civil-service employee in the Navy Materiel Redistribution and Disposal Office—NMRDO. Translation: the Navy needed to get rid of a lot of trucks.

My mother was thrilled that I was in the civil service. I'd have a steady job, and those had not been easy to come by in our family. Even better, because it was the civil service, it wasn't easy to terminate anyone's employment. There was just one small problem: I probably should have been terminated before I even began, because I was spectacularly incompetent as a file clerk. As months passed, however, and people left the office, I somehow was moved into increasingly more senior positions, at one point finding myself the chief file clerk. Since I spent much of my time daydreaming about performing or fantasizing about the last movie I'd seen, not much got filed. It got so bad that one day everything stopped while all the naval officers did the filing. Eventually even the civil service caught on and I was gently demoted to a less senior position.

In the midst of my brief foray into the world of filing, I was still performing in the tap chorus for Mrs. Curry, and during one performance at an Atlanta hotel I met the man who would change my life. It was the start of a pattern repeated throughout the years: imperfect as my relations were with many of the key men in my life, it was sometimes they who gave me the courage to really take chances. In this case it was Herb Shriner, a comic actor and raconteur in the vein of Will Rogers.

Herb would tell funny, homespun stories about life in his fictional Indiana hometown, chatting in a low-key style with an aw-shucks, deadpan drawl—he even played the harmonica. He was a little bit Will Rogers, a little bit Garrison Keillor, good-looking and utterly charming. He had worked as a performer with the USO and eventually went on to become a radio and television personality with his own television show, *Herb Shriner Time*. When we met he was playing a local Atlanta nightclub, and during his time in town, he happened to catch one of the Curry troupe performances. When I came on for my specialty song, he was smitten and asked me out to lunch. I was smitten right back, and we started going out constantly during the couple of weeks he was in Atlanta. I was thrilled to be dating a professional performer, and the romance of being with a man in show business added to his allure.

Soon enough I was in love for the first time, and it underscored my hunger to move on with my life and pursue the destiny I'd been dreaming of since I was a movie-mad child. Herb had to leave Atlanta, but we kept in touch through letters. It was 1948, and I was twenty years old, convinced that my future, whatever it was to be, lay outside of Atlanta. I had by this time acquired another deadly secretarial job, this time for the Federal Housing Administration, and when my mother suggested that we take a two-week vacation in New York, I jumped at the chance. I was ecstatic at the idea of spending time in Manhattan, only I wasn't so sure about the trip's two-week limit.

My mother had a friend whose brother lived uptown, near Columbia University, in a rambling apartment with plenty of room for guests. His two sons were away at school, so my mother and I were invited to stay; I'm sure we couldn't have afforded the trip otherwise. As we were preparing to leave Atlanta, my mother noticed that I was packing rather heavily for a two-week vacation. The fact was, I wanted to remain in New York, and I hesitantly told my mother that's what I was contemplating. I don't think she believed I was really serious, but in the end I packed just about every piece of clothing I owned. I didn't know if I'd have the courage to actually stay in New York, but I knew that Herb Shriner was in New York, and I was in love with Herb Shriner. I also realized that any possibility of pursuing a career in theater could only materialize if I took my chances in the unquestioned center of theater in the United States: New York City. I was ready.

Mother and I spent the two weeks in February as most tourists did, and still do, seeing the traditional sights. Herb was rehearsing a Broadway revue called *Inside U.S.A.*, which opened in April of 1948, starring Beatrice Lillie. As the days passed, my conviction to stay grew, and I even went on a couple of auditions. Arthur Godfrey told me that I had a lovely voice, but his television show already had too many singers. I was, however, quickly learning that you need to take advantage of any possible contacts you make, no matter how remote, and our host up near Columbia was friendly with a woman who was the switchboard operator at the Irving Berlin publishing offices. She arranged for me to sing for Helmy Kresa, a songwriter and arranger for Mr. Berlin. I chose "Smoke Gets in Your Eyes," and Mr. Kresa's reaction is imprinted in my memory bank to this day: "You have a really pretty voice, but you don't sing with feeling. You've got to learn to do that." Sixty years later that piece of advice has informed my entire professional mission.

Oh, how I loved New York! And, oh, how I loved discovering that the city seemed to run on nickels. A nickel would get you a phone call, a ride on the subway, entrance to one of the locked toilets at Rockefeller Center, and a ride on the Staten Island Ferry. I took that ride to Staten Island twice, just for the sheer fun of it. Holy Hannah, I was in NEW YORK CITY!

As the time approached for our return to Atlanta, I grew firmer in my conviction that I was going to stay. It wasn't just that I wanted to live in Manhattan; I simply knew that I belonged nowhere else but in Manhattan. New York City meant boundless opportunity, and I knew, with absolute certainty, that if I didn't try to find a way to sing it would be a terrible waste of talent, opportunity, and life. That I had at least one friend in New York, Herb, probably bucked me up, for in truth I didn't have an overwhelming confidence in my talent. I knew what I wanted to do with my life, but it still seemed almost unfathomable that I could actually make it happen. I was much younger than my twenty years in oh-so-many ways: I had, after all, been sleeping in bed with my mother for most of my life, including, on this exciting, anxious, and life-altering trip to the big city.

The man who had hosted our visit agreed to allow me to stay on in his apartment with him for a few more months, and I broke the news to my mother that I was determined to remain. I remember standing on the platform at Penn Station, watching my mother board her train back to Atlanta. She was clearly devastated and worried about me. I had been her life, day in and day out, for twenty years. I was an extension of her—her arm, her leg—I belonged to her. Completely.

We were now about to live nearly a thousand miles apart, but her attempts to cajole me into returning with her were useless. The truth is, I was so happy at the prospect of independence and a life in New York that I did not give much thought to my mother's state of mind. For the first time in my life I felt free. Despite any anxieties and fears, I had a strong will—if I hadn't, by this point my mother would have subsumed me entirely. I was, I realize now, more than a little ruthless in my determination. There was no way my mother could have stopped me from staying, short of handcuffing me and dragging me onto the train behind her. I don't remember seeing her cry, but she must have on the way home. As a mother myself, I can imagine how frightened and sad she must have been on that train back to Atlanta, but back then I had one all-encompassing thought: I was in New York with the possibility of an exciting future ahead of me.

I was in love with Herb, but it was never a serious love affair from his perspective. In the beginning he was clearly attracted to me and made all the moves, but I was truly crazy about him—he was my first love. I didn't know what the hell I was doing. I was incredibly naïve, very needy, and, probably because of my father having left, still had an overwhelming desire to be loved, cared for, and protected. I can remember actually saying to Herb: "Please love me." If there's a phrase that is sure to make a guy run, that's gotta be it. I remember the moment I said it, thinking that it was the wrong thing to say. It's embarrassing to admit, and embarrassing to remember, but it's also the truth. I was one very young, impressionable, naïve young woman. Eventually Herb got married and had two boys, one of whom he named after Will Rogers—Wil Shriner.

With or without Herb, I was on my own, yet not at all lonely. I had few acquaintances, and was by myself much of the time, but I was having a love affair with the city, overwhelmed with a sense of freedom and exhilaration. I had never been away from home before—I hadn't gone to college—so this was the first time that my life belonged completely to me.

I'd wake up at dawn and just lose myself wandering the streets as the city was coming to life. I would stop at diners and have a cup of coffee, which I imagined to be a very adult thing to do. The sounds of the city delighted me—even the early-morning groans of the garbage trucks seemed musical to me. The winter of 1948 proved to be particularly frigid, and snow from a December blizzard was still piled up along the sidewalks. But even the cold held an enchantment for me, since I knew with absolute certainty that I was finally where I belonged.

I belonged in New York in a way I never had in Atlanta. Even as a small girl, I had never understood segregation—it literally made no sense to me. Separate water fountains labeled "white" and "colored"? Segregated seating on the bus? When "colored" help came to work in a white person's house, they had to bring their own dishes and glasses if they wanted to eat or drink. This struck me as not only nonsensical, but also completely horrible. So did any racist talk: when I went back to the office where I had been working in order to say goodbye, my boss actually said to me: "I don't want to see you walking down the street with a Nigra or a Jew." Surrounded as I was by such attitudes, I'm not even sure why my own feelings were so different right from the start. I suspect my father's example was a major influence on my thinking, because I never heard him utter a single racist or anti-Semitic word. In his job as a salesman he reported directly to his Jewish brother-in-law, a man he liked and respected a great deal.

Atlanta is now a far more cosmopolitan city than it was in the 1940s, but some attitudes die slowly; forty-three years after I left Atlanta, I returned in June of 1995 for my fiftieth high school reunion. I was standing at the hotel desk when a classmate gave me a friendly holler from down the hall. We talked a bit about our lives—superficial friendly reunion chatter. My career, my life in New York. Her life in Georgia. Bonds renewed. Until, with a big smile, she casually exclaimed, "Barbara, you talk just like a Jew!" I was left completely speechless.

All the time I had felt I was an outsider who didn't belong in Atlanta, I thought there must be something wrong with me. Now, after years in New York, I came to realize that there was something wrong with them. That sounds a little more dismissive than I mean it to. I have great friends in Georgia—terrific people. It's just that life there feels right for them, I suppose, but definitely not for me.

My God, when I think what my life might have been like had I not had the courage to stay in New York. There are others who are so very talented but for some reason or other don't have the courage or the strength to take the chance, to put themselves on the line. There's no question that I was putting myself on the line back in 1948—even when I couldn't even locate exactly where the line was.

New York was still amply stocked with grand old movie palaces in those days, and I couldn't stay away. At the Strand or the Paramount you could get a whole evening's entertainment for fifty cents. There would be a first-run movie, and oftentimes one of the truly great big bands—Tommy Dorsey's or Glenn Miller's—and some of the best vaudeville acts in the country. I saw Bill Robinson dance again, and this time was astonished by his gifts. At one performance I attended, Josephine Baker made an electrifying entrance that I'll never forget, slinking onstage dragging a full-length white mink coat behind her. One of the stranger and more memorable acts was a comedienne who came on dressed primly in a smart suit, hat, gloves, and a fur stole. At the end of her act she daintily removed the stole, set it down on the stage, and watched as it walked off—yes, a live dog had been wrapped around her neck the whole time. It was one of the funniest things I'd ever seen.

I loved walking down the street, catching snatches of overlapping conversations conducted in an enticing mix of multiple languages. I discovered rice pudding, an exotic delicacy to me—oh, how I loved the taste and texture of it. One day I decided that it was high time I got drunk—another adult indulgence I'd never met Jeanne Meganck, a lovely young Belgian girl who had worked for Sabena Airlines and was now working for Christian Dior. She moved into the apartment, taking over the daughter's bed. I was paying forty dollars a month to my stingy landlady. Forty dollars out of a total monthly pay of $160 from Shell Oil. Of course I still had it better than Jeanne; knowing that Jeanne worked for Christian Dior, the landlady charged her fifty. Did Mrs. Scrooge think we wouldn't share that knowledge?

Jeanne, who was a hell of a lot more worldly-wise than I, summed up the situation pretty quickly, and when the mother went away for a week's vacation, locking the phone before her departure so that we couldn't use it in her absence, Jeanne and I reached our collective breaking point. Jeanne began to look for another place the two of us could share and through a connection at Dior found a beautiful apartment in a brownstone in the East Thirties. She also found a third person to share the apartment with us, another Belgian girl, named Mip VanderWaaren. Mip was nice, but the apartment was spectacular. We couldn't believe our good fortune. There were two bedrooms, a small one for Mip and a larger one that Jeanne and I shared. Oversized windows filled the bedrooms in the back with sunshine, and the front featured a large salon furnished with very beautiful French country antiques. We had struck pay dirt.

Almost every weekend the apartment was filled with Sabena pilots and flight attendants stopping over between flights. The war had ended only three years before, and although everyone wanted to put the war behind them, occasionally the subject would arise.

The bravery displayed during the war by women who were only slighter older than I astonished me. One of the women who visited us sometimes was a childhood friend of Jeanne's who had

tried before. In the apartment where I was staying I found a bottle of Manischewitz, the sweet kosher wine, and one night proceeded to consume it all by myself, just because I could. Some years later, both wine and food would become serious problems for me, but in those exhilarating first days in New York, I was drunk on the city itself.

I WAS ON my own at last, but with one not so insignificant problem: money. I had arrived in New York with the seventy-five dollars that I'd saved up from my job in Atlanta, and it was quickly being spent on movies, coffee, and rice pudding. As excited as I was about having made it to the city of my dreams, I didn't know how I was going to survive there.

I went to work for Asiatic Petroleum, a subsidiary of Shell Oil, sometime in the summer of 1948. As part of the job I typed lots of letters to Caracas and Maracaibo. Those faraway places seemed dramatic and glamorous to me, although the glamour quickly vanished on the days when I just typed rows and rows of numbers for eight consecutive soul-deadening hours. (In later years I did have a more satisfying temp job reading applications from people applying for a Fulbright scholarship. It was actually fascinating to rea about people's dreams. They may not have been show-busine dreams, but they interested me mightily.)

When my landlord's sons came back from school, this gener man, understandably enough, needed my bedroom. I answer classified ad in the *New York Times* and moved in with a m and daughter whose apartment on the corner of Eighth Aven Fifty-second Street lay on the northernmost edge of the T District. The three of us slept in the one bedroom in three s beds, until the daughter got married and moved out. That' lived in Brussels near Jeanne during the war. When, in those days, Jeanne would occasionally ask her where she disappeared to from time to time, it became clear to Jeanne that she was not to ask any more questions. After the war this young woman was decorated by all of the Allied nations; she had saved the lives of many Allied airmen who had lost their planes over Nazi-controlled territory. Those who survived the downing of their planes would be guided to safety by this young woman, undertaking nighttime journeys through Belgium and France to Portugal and safety. Ponce de Leon Avenue in Atlanta began to seem very, very far away.

I quickly felt stuck at Asiatic Petroleum, so I invented a very satisfying escape. I had learned about the old films that were shown at the Museum of Modern Art, and one afternoon as I was plodding through all of those numbers, I remembered that there was a Rudolph Valentino silent playing at the Modern. I went into the ladies' room, rubbed spit on my mascara and daubed it under my eyes, and, trying to look suitably peaked, told them I was feeling dreadfully ill. Off I went to have my first experience with The Sheik. Heaven.

When I worked for Shell Oil we were on the top floor in one of the tallest buildings in Rockefeller Center. I loved gazing out at the view, taking special note of the light in winter, that deep, rich, radiant blue just before nightfall. There was a sense of camaraderie with my coworkers, and after hours we would wander to a nearby bar and have drinks. I would sit at the bar, singing snatches of arias from opera. I really didn't know much about opera despite all those years of listening to the Metropolitan Opera radio broadcasts, but I remember singing *"Una furtiva lagrima,"* the beautiful tenor aria from *L'Elisir d'Amore* just because I thought it was a pretty tune. Ditto for the "Habanera" from *Carmen*. Because I worked in Rockefeller Center I was eligible to join the Rockefeller Center Choristers and was thrilled when I was accepted. The chorus director said I had the most beautiful voice he had ever worked with; and, starved as I was for a chance to sing, his words came like manna from heaven. The Choristers often sang in the outdoor skating rink under the big statue of Atlas, and sometimes our performances were televised. Nelson Rockefeller visited us during rehearsal one day—such was life in the big city, and I was gobbling it up.

In the fall of 1948 I performed in the Shell in-house review *Shellebrities*. Or to be more accurate, I performed in, choreographed, and directed *Shellebrities*. I grabbed any theatrical work I could. It was a chance to learn.

It was also at this very time that one of the dichotomies in my performing career was beginning to emerge full-blown: as much as I loved to sing, I was terrified of auditioning. On the one hand, I had faith in my talent; but, on the other, I felt extreme anxiety about actually performing. I've always been a nervous human being, so much so that I've often marveled that I ever really got into this business. I was terrified about meeting people, and simply greeting a prospective agent would leave me sweating profusely.

In fact, sweating profusely—*hyperhidrosis* is the medical term—had been a problem for me ever since I was an adolescent. In school I used to have to put a piece of paper over the test paper so the sweat wouldn't drip down and blur my answers. When I was asked to go to the blackboard to work out a math problem, I would be so nervous that the perspiration would run down my arm and drip off my elbow. I remember once having on a short-sleeved sweater and sweating so much that there were puddles at the top of my skirt from the perspiration running down my arms. Even after I began performing on Broadway, I used to have all sorts of extra material placed underneath my costumes so that the moisture wouldn't show.

But much as I feared auditioning, my determination to succeed proved to be even greater, and when I met a woman named Teddy who gave voice lessons, she helped me put together audition material. It was surprisingly easy to audition in those days: you just looked in the show-business periodicals that came out and then showed up at the time and place indicated.

In the fall of 1949 I was offered a job at a very nice supper club in Boston called the Darbury Room. The owners had something new in mind for their room and I had no way of knowing, nor did they, if this would last. I was scared, but I finally decided to take the job after getting a two-week leave of absence from Asiatic Petroleum. What if the show flopped? What if I lost my job at Asiatic Petroleum? I'm afraid I didn't care one hoot about the problems of Asiatic Petroleum, but I did care about having enough money to pay the rent.

Off I went to Boston, where Erwin Straus, the son of the operetta composer Oscar Straus, had come up with the idea of putting together a revue of songs dedicated to a single musical-theater composer. He was to be the musical director and pianist, and I was one of four singers in the cast of two women and two men. What we did were "tab shows" (short "tabloid" performances) based on the work of a different composer each time: Richard Rodgers, Jerome Kern, George Gershwin, Cole Porter, Irving Berlin. These types of revues are more common now—Broadway shows have been built around the catalogues of Duke Ellington (*Sophisticated Ladies*) and Johnny Mercer (*Dream*)—but it was a fresh idea at the time, and I really lucked out. These shows were all

based on material for which I was particularly well suited. The
first show centered on the work of Jerome Kern, and I realized
that because his songs were all written for musicals, the format allowed me to perform them as if in a mini–musical comedy, rather
than just sing in the usual nightclub style. Audiences loved the
shows, which meant that the owners loved the shows. When it
became clear that the run would last, I placed a call to Asiatic Petroleum: "I'm afraid I won't be coming back." Someone else could
check those numbers—and play hooky at the Museum of Modern
Art. I was now officially working in show business!

I stayed in Boston for nine very happy months doing these
shows, and without really knowing it I was receiving extremely
valuable experience. I was learning how to connect with an audience, and in the process was singing the very best material ever
written for musical theater. With only four of us in each show, we
all had a chance to shine. I even received my first, if slightly ge-
neric, notice in *Variety*: "Barbara Cook proves an actress as well
as a singer and dancer." Not exactly an ecstatic rave, but I was
the first performer mentioned, and it was a nice start. More meaningful to me were the enthusiastic responses from the audiences
and my castmates, all of which gave me some much-needed confidence. With each successive revue, I began stretching my range,
singing songs it would never have occurred to me to try, like Ethel
Merman's songs from *Annie Get Your Gun*. I started to tell myself:
"You could really have a shot at this." I listen back now to some
of my early singing, and I did not know how good I was. Good in
the sense of having a really pretty sound. Not put-together yet, but
really sweet, a very pretty voice. I started to acquire the glimmer
of a personal style—an individual way of phrasing.

While in Boston I lived in the Charlotte Cushman Club.

Charlotte Cushman was the first American actress to achieve international renown, at a time when acting was looked upon as a somewhat dubious profession for a young lady. The Cushman Clubs that existed in various cities had been founded so that touring actresses would have somewhere safe and respectable to stay when they were performing in that town. The rooms were tiny, but there was a communal kitchen. Boston was, of course, a big tryout town at this time, so the club was full of women in shows. I remember that the actresses sort of looked down on those of us who weren't in the legitimate theater: "We are of the *theater*, and you're just singing in a *club*."

When the show at the Darbury eventually closed I hung on in Boston for a little while; I had quit my job in New York, after all, and had nothing solid waiting back in Manhattan. During the run in Boston I'd also had my first television experience when Tommy O'Neal and I were asked to perform on a variety show for WBZ television. Tommy played piano and I sang, and we also shared a few duets. Fear gripped me again at the thought of this entirely new medium, especially since I was required to read the promotional commercials as well, but somehow we stumbled through. Unfortunately the television show soon came to an end and things pretty quickly got tight for me financially. I can recall several weeks at the Cushman Club when I subsisted only on apples and Milky Way candy bars, and I had to wire my father to send some money to tide me over.

Bereft of prospects or not, I eventually had to return to New York. But as luck would have it, I was introduced to the great composer Vernon Duke, who took me under his wing after hearing me sing. Vernon had left Russia as Vladimir Dukelsky and changed his name at the suggestion of George Gershwin. As Vernon Duke, he had written some of the greatest popular songs of the twentieth century: "April in Paris," "I Can't Get Started," "Taking a Chance on Love," and "Autumn in New York." Vernon was one of the first people who believed in me, and he liked my voice so much that he asked me to sing at backers' auditions, which are informal performances used to drum up investors for new Broadway shows. He also introduced me to all sorts of exotic experiences—like eating artichokes. Before Vernon, I had never even seen an artichoke, much less learned how to eat one.

It was also Vernon who literally changed my life when he urged me to audition for the 1950 season at Tamiment, the summer resort in the Pocono Mountains of Pennsylvania. My job, along with fellow members of the "social staff," was to provide entertainment for the guests, most of whom were young office workers from New York who came to the Poconos for their two-week summer vacation. Plane travel was still very expensive in 1950, and Europe and the Caribbean were out of reach for most. At Tamiment, however, these office workers paid one flat fee for their entire stay, and after entering the gate, everything was taken care of—no need to carry any money. There was golf, tennis, swimming, canoeing, archery, and three delicious meals a day, plus snacks. A small orchestra played for dancing in the evening. It was a great deal for the guests, and a terrific learning experience for the social staff.

I don't remember much about my audition for Tamiment, except that it was in somebody's apartment, quite informal, and it was the first time I met Jerry Bock. Jerry was a brilliant composer who went on to write *She Loves Me* and *Fiddler on the Roof,* and also to win a Pulitzer Prize for *Fiorello!* He was the main composer at Tamiment during this period, and, as I would learn, an extraordinary artist with a great gift for melody. He was working at this time with the lyricist Larry Holofcener, and together they, along with George Weiss, went on to write the score for the Broadway musical *Mr. Wonderful*, starring Sammy Davis, Jr. I got the job and, as it turned out, would spend the next two summers at Tamiment, working with an extraordinary group of gifted, indeed brilliant, artists.

It was at Tamiment that I met Jack Cassidy, my future costar in *She Loves Me*. I remember being distinctly awed when I was told that Jack had already been in something like twenty-one Broadway shows, because I, at that point, had exactly one nightclub engagement in Boston to my credit. Oh, what a character Jack was! The first thing you noticed about Jack was that he was beautiful. I don't mean handsome, but *beautiful*. Almost too pretty. He didn't look especially strong because of it and was told sometimes, "You're too pretty for the role." He was also quite a dandy. He was so aware of his clothes and of everything related to his physical appearance: I recall that he used to put toilet paper under his shirt collar so that it would roll perfectly! That's the sort of thing he would do all the time. For the Tamiment season I was to be the ingénue and Jack my leading man, and we performed little scenes and songs that Jerry and Larry had written. All of the material was completely original, and it amazed me how quickly Jerry could write a song.

Tamiment is also where I first met Herbert Ross, who went on to such great acclaim for his work with Barbra Streisand on the film version of *Funny Girl* and as director of the films *The Turning Point* and *Steel Magnolias*. In a further stroke of good luck I also met Joe Stein, who went on to write the terrific book for *Fiddler*. What a dear, dear man. He was one of the creators of the first show I starred in, *Plain and Fancy*, and Tamiment was the start of a fifty-year friendship that continued until he died in 2014. He was a very sweet man and oh so funny. One day while I was very pregnant with my son, Adam, I ran into Joe at Variety Arts Studios, where I was about to take an acting class with my then husband, David. Joe took one look at my belly and even before greeting me wisecracked: "If you're not pregnant, you're one very sick woman!"

I wanted to make the most of my chance in 1950, and that's what scared the hell out of me. I knew that performing at Tamiment wasn't just a good summer job—it was potentially a career-launching situation. *Your Show of Shows* with Sid Caesar was really born at Tamiment; all the writers who went on to create that landmark show had worked at Tamiment the summer immediately before mine; and my bunk mate—we always had bunk mates—was Lucille Kallen, the only woman in that group of writers for Sid Caesar. I have a memory of wandering by the lake one day and meeting a young writer named Neil Simon, as he sat with his soon-to-be wife, Joan. Neil was just a kid—absolutely no fame yet. It's astounding to realize how many successful writers and performers received their start at Tamiment.

Scared as I was about Tamiment, once I got there I didn't really have time to fret over my insecurities because we were too busy working; every week for the ten weeks of summer, the company, which included singers, comedians, and a chorus, would have to put on an entirely new variety show. We rehearsed all week and performed for the guests on Friday and Saturday nights. In addition, on Wednesdays there was an informal show where any of us could get up and do whatever we wanted. I loved it.

The atmosphere at Tamiment was inspiring, and the resort itself was a wonderful place. On Sundays, our one day off, we could take a boat on the lake or attempt to master archery. The countryside was beautiful and the food was tremendous—this Southern gal quickly discovered the unending delights of brisket, stuffed derma, matzoh balls, gefilte fish, and schmaltz you could spread on bread like it was butter. Jewish soul food. Healthy, maybe not, but heavenly—yes! Room and board were part of the deal, and because virtually everything was taken care of (unless you wanted an extra meal), if you watched your pennies you could save five hundred dollars from a summer of work—a tremendous amount of money to me then, and more than enough to help me hang on to my half of my apartment back in New York. At the end of the 1951 theater season, I had the five hundred I had saved from my first Broadway show, *Flahooley*, plus that five hundred from the Tamiment season. This meant that for the first time in my life I had a thousand bucks. Wow!

Needless to say, room and board were high on my list of priorities, but the most vital aspect of working at Tamiment was the confidence it gave me. I gradually got used to the idea that I *belonged* on the stage with people who had performed in Broadway musicals. That was a big deal for me, and while I still wasn't entirely at home onstage, working with all these people who had real careers—men and women who constantly encouraged me—gave me new confidence.

That summer at Tamiment led directly to my first New York nightclub engagement. Max Gordon, who owned the Blue Angel—a trendy supper club—with Herbert Jacoby, made a habit of coming up to Tamiment to check out the talent on our informal variety nights. When he saw me perform, he told me that I should come to the club and audition as soon as I got back to town. This was a real break, because the Blue Angel, just like Tamiment, held a special place as an important springboard for emerging talent. Thursdays were their audition days: you walked in, they listened to you. I hurried down to the Blue Angel on the very first Thursday I was back in town and when I'd finished singing the owners hired me on the spot.

There was just one problem: the currently scheduled performer was not working out and as the last-minute replacement, I was to open in precisely four days. I was ecstatic but stunned, not to mention terrified. I didn't have an act and had only one weekend to put some songs together. I rushed home and got on the phone to a pianist I knew. Luckily he wasn't doing much that weekend and we went right to work, all the while bearing in mind the only piece of advice Max had given me: "Whatever you do, don't sing 'The Boy Next Door.' I'm sick of it!"

We worked like hell through the weekend and put together about a half hour of material, which proved to be just enough; at the Blue Angel four acts would perform two short sets each night, so you weren't doing a whole solo evening. I was sharing the bill with comedian Wally Cox, a group called the 3 Mad-Moiselles, and the folk quartet the Weavers. A full concert it wasn't, but it was still thirty minutes onstage by myself, and I latched on to the opportunity with great determination. In the process, I also chose some material that now strikes me as downright bizarre—whatever possessed me to sing "It Ain't Necessarily So" from *Porgy and Bess*?

Fortunately I also made some more suitable choices, including Rodgers and Hart's "Little Girl Blue." *Variety* took notice, referring to me as a "blonde cutie, in her early twenties, who evidences potential with a vocal style and a routine that still can't qualify as an 'act' but will be heard from in time." After having only four days of preparation I was very happy with that review, and when audiences proved to be enthusiastic, Max invited me to return for another engagement.

One night during that initial run, one of the Weavers asked me to join him between shows for a meal just around the corner at Hamburger Heaven. The Weavers were a known commodity at the time, having scored some hit singles, including "Goodnight, Irene." I was happy to go out for a hamburger, but before we went he cautioned me that I should really think twice about it because the FBI already suspected the Weavers of being Communists. It would be just a few years later that two of the Weavers were called before the House Un-American Activities Committee. I was still quite naïve at the time, but I wasn't afraid of having a hamburger with this nice man.

When the Blue Angel engagement ended I found myself out of work and dangerously low on money. I toured briefly in a tab show that proved a real education because we opened this show in a tiny Kentucky club that was situated right near a gambling casino. It was really rough, with lots of Mafia people on the scene. It was actually more than rough—it was downright scary. Clearly, it was a long way from Broadway. Eventually the tour ended and once again I was without work, but it was then, just when my prospects looked particularly bleak, that my Tamiment friend Jack Cassidy came to the rescue.

Jack was in between shows at the time, and he had an uncle who was the postmaster in Flushing, Queens. The holidays were approaching, and they always hired extra help to deal with the influx of Christmas cards. Once again I found myself back in an office situation—fortunately for the very last time—where I did grunt work while Jack, as I recall, did a lot of swanning about while looking important and doing very little work. He was a thoroughly charming man, and incredibly funny and clever. He was, however, not the kind of guy who was going to settle down to hard work in a post office if he could help it.

I'm not sure how many of those Christmas cards were sorted properly, because as a post office employee I was a great singer. But, it was shortly thereafter that I auditioned for the show that became my first official Broadway credit, the wonderfully strange musical *Flahooley*. My agent Charlie Baker, a very elegant man who became head of William Morris's theatrical department and worked as my agent for over twenty years, sent me on the audition for *Flahooley*. The audition was held at the Martin Beck Theatre on Forty-fifth Street, and I, who feared and hated auditions, had one of the happiest auditions of my life, thanks to E. Y. ("Yip") Harburg.

I knew Yip's work, of course, as the lyricist of *Finian's Rainbow* and *The Wizard of Oz*. I auditioned singing "My Funny Valentine," a piece I often used for auditions. As soon as I was finished, a little man came roaring up onto the stage and threw his arms around me in obvious delight—it was like being given a bear hug by Santa Claus—and that is how I officially met Yip Harburg. He was an adorable-looking man with a great smile—a charming, charming man. A lot of people thought he was difficult to work with but I never found him remotely difficult. He held very strong opinions that were considered pretty radical for the times. He took on racism in *Finian's Rainbow*, and his work was almost always socially conscious. Working with the composer Jay Gorney, he wrote the song "Brother, Can You Spare a Dime?" about down-and-out men in the Depression.

In an illustration of how you can't put people in boxes and always expect them to behave in a preordained fashion, Jay Gorney's wife, Edalaine, had left her husband and married Yipper in 1943. It proved to be a real scandal at the time, but Eddie, as Yip called her, was a very warm, sweet woman and they had a terrific marriage. Yip was such a generous, warm man; that's why my audition for *Flahooley* was a dream. I had the show the very moment the audition concluded, although I didn't know it then. To this day it remains the only time an audition unfolded in such a magical fashion for me—and the ease of that experience nearly ruined me!

In truth, my involvement with *Flahooley* actually dated back a little earlier, although I didn't realize it at the time. I had taken to dropping in at a private midtown spot called the Gold Key Club, and Colin Romoff, who was the club's piano player, would call me whenever Judy Garland stopped by just to sing for friends and her own amusement. Judy was a very big influence on my singing—oh, how I wanted to sing like her, but it was impossible. My voice teacher said to me: "Forget it. You have a completely different voice. You're a soprano." But listening to Judy taught me how a song must contain a beginning, a middle, and an end—that it should possess an unbroken line both musically and lyrically, while taking the listener on an emotional journey. To hear her sing "By Myself" in that intimate room was the thrill of a lifetime.

During her first storied run at the Palace in 1951–52, I went to see her repeatedly. My agent knew Judy and wanted to take me backstage to meet her but I just couldn't. I thought I would die if I met her—I was simply too much in awe of her. I did eventually meet her later in the run, and she was very cordial, but I remained in awe of her.

The one other major influence on my singing was Mabel Mercer, who didn't have much of a voice but used words better than any other singer I can think of. Mabel communicated the richness of good lyrics, the subtext lying beneath the surface. She did things other singers wouldn't—she would really lay into consonants instead of vowels. Mabel would sing the word "wonderful" and lay into that "n" in the middle of the word, which gave it a completely different sound and meaning than a smoothly sung, skimming-the-surface "wonderful." My own attention to consonants really comes from Mabel's influence—I always want to be understood and never want to overdo.

At some point I started singing for fun at the Gold Key Club, and one night the composer Sammy Fain stopped me after my performance and mentioned that he was working on a show that I'd be perfect for—*Flahooley*. It was well after this encounter at the Gold Key that I actually auditioned for *Flahooley*, and because the audition had gone so well, I was not completely surprised when Charlie Baker called and said, "Are you sitting down? *You got the show!*" I'd been in New York three years by now, and my dream of performing in a Broadway musical was going to come true.

I had no idea, however, of how painful I'd find the process of putting a new show together. When rehearsals began early in 1951 I was so awkward and green that I was embarrassed to even mime picking up a glass or opening a door. What saved me was that I could sing the hell out of that score—I knew just what I was doing with the singing. The acting was a completely different story.

As a result of my insecurities I started developing all sorts of nervous ailments when we took the show out of town. I decided that every other girl in the show was prettier than I was, that every other girl could act better than I could (which may have been true), and that every other girl could sing better than I could (which definitely was not the case). By the time we arrived in Philadelphia for the out-of-town tryout, I was positive they were going to fire me any day and move somebody from the chorus into my ingénue role. Net result? Physical ailments started springing up, and I developed a hypersensitivity on my hip and leg, to the point where I had to sleep on top of the covers. This all became so emotionally painful that I remember coming back to my hotel one night in Philadelphia and saying to myself, "If this is what it means to do musical comedy, I don't want any part of it. I will never do this again."

I was so beset by anxiety over my total lack of acting experience that rehearsals continued to be a trial by fire. How did I overcome my fears? I didn't. I simply distracted myself from them by eating. By this point in my life I had already been struggling with my weight for several years, finding it, as most people do, a lot easier to put on than take off. By the time I was in rehearsal for *Flahooley* I had already acquired the habit of knowing exactly what I weighed at any point in my life. *Flahooley*, 136 pounds. A chubby 136 at that. A photo announcing my casting in the show found me looking decidedly more zaftig than the ideal Broadway ingénue.

I found a White Castle burger joint in Philadelphia and made it my secret refuge. Whenever my nerves over my inexperience got the better of me, that's where I ran. I'd tell myself, "You know you shouldn't be doing this. You know you cannot afford to gain any weight." And then I'd order a sack full of those little White Castle hamburgers. The next night I'd do the same.

The problem became acute. I was a little too big to begin with, and I started getting bigger. And then I heard about a doctor who could help out with this kind of problem, and I was introduced to Dexedrine. At the time it seemed a godsend: here was a little pill that didn't just help curb your appetite, it also put you in a state of great creative ferment. You know how some days you feel particularly creative, your mind is clicking, and you have incredible energy? Energy-to-clean-your-entire-house kind of energy? That's what Dexedrine brought. It was a wonderful thing. Too bad it turned out to be so terrible for you.

As for *Flahooley*, as many lovers of obscure Broadway musicals know, it proved to be among the most peculiar shows to open in the 1950s. First, Yip switched the title of the show from *Toyland* to *Flahooley* after the dolls that are at the center of the plot. (Yip once quipped that he chose that kooky title because "it's the only name we could think of that you can't spell backwards.") The musical was set in Capsulanti, Indiana, where the B. G. Bigelow company manufactures toys. My role was that of Sandy, a puppet operator at the factory, who is in love with the puppet designer, Sylvester, played by Jerome Courtland. Sylvester has created a fabulous new doll for the Christmas season, one that can blow bubble gum, read comics, and let out belly laughs. It will put the fortunes of Bigelow and Sandy and Sylvester into the stratosphere—until a competitor copies the doll and undercuts the price.

Meanwhile, an emissary from Arabia has come to Bigelow to have Aladdin's magic lamp repaired. This is where the singer Yma Sumac entered the picture. Born in Peru—the rumors that she was really Amy Camus from Brooklyn were simply not true—Yma was endowed with a truly amazing voice with an almost unbelievable range. I remember standing in the wings during performances and listening to the astounding things she could do with her voice. She had the amazing ability to slide all the way up to the top of her range and then sing a glissando all the way down. When she did the glissando down she sang two notes at the same time, like double-stops on a violin. The conductor, Maurice Levine, and I could never figure out how she did it. "What has she got in there instead of vocal cords?" I would wonder. She didn't really sing songs—she sang special material that her husband, Moises, would write for her. And there she was, in the middle of Capsulanti, Indiana.

Yip had heard Yma sing and been knocked out, so the already crazy plot of *Flahooley* became a whole lot more complicated in order to include Yma's character of Najla, an emissary from Arabia. And just how did the Arabs come to Capsulanti, Indiana? Because just as the fortunes of Bigelow are faltering, due to the cheaper imitation flahooleys being produced by a rival, Sylvester puts one of the doll's hands on Aladdin's lamp and out pops a genie named Abou Ben Atom. I told you there was a lot of plot . . . Well, the genie promises to grant Sylvester any wish he desires, and the next thing you know the flahooleys are rushing off the assembly line, causing a flood in the market and a subsequent collapse. Unemployment skyrockets in the town of Capsulanti, and soon mobs are burning piles of flahooleys in the town square. Somehow it all ends happily.

Oy vey, as we used to say on Peachtree Street.

This was not exactly your average Broadway musical. To tell the truth, while I can relate the basic plot of the show, I didn't know then exactly what it was all supposed to be about. I was so green that I would just look at my stuff and think, "How do I make this work?" I didn't and couldn't see the overall picture. Both Yip and Sammy Fain had pronounced liberal leanings, and just as they had condemned racism in *Finian's Rainbow*, *Flahooley*, too, had a subversive, anticapitalist message embedded within all the whimsy. I don't think I grasped it fully at the time, but it seemed to have been written with the burgeoning resistance to the atomic power movement in mind, not to mention a desire to comment on the witch hunts beginning to take place as McCarthyism swept through Washington; it was the genie hunts and burning of the dolls within the plot that the creators hoped would speak to this shameful chapter in our country's history. And, just to make sure no sacred cow was left untouched, *Flahooley* even took on Christmas! The song "Sing the Merry," which wasn't recorded, satirized the rampant commercialization of the holiday. Here's the last line: "And for Christ's sake may this nation soon give Christmas back to Christ." That didn't make it past Philadelphia.

I was trying to learn my part, figure out the show, and overcome my overwhelming nerves; but at the same time that I was riddled with insecurity, I also possessed an unwavering core of self-confidence about how I wanted to sing a song. I feared I was going to be replaced at any moment, yet I still had total belief in my approach to a song. Now get this. The first time I listened to the orchestral accompaniment, I heard a recurring saxophone line that interfered with my phrasing. So I asked our conductor to change the sax line. He said, no, we couldn't do that. So, I said, "Look— they hired me to do my thing, and I can't do it with that sax interfering." I fought for it, and whadda ya know? It was changed!

One day I was once again standing in the wings, nervous as hell, and for some reason it occurred to me that what I had to do was search for the authentic essence of myself and communicate that—find what was intrinsically mine. There's only one of me, so there could be no real competition with anyone else. If I sang from my authentic self, then I was only in competition with myself, and with the journey I had set for me and the song. Suddenly a great weight was lifted off my shoulders. That moment in the wings marked the beginning of Barbara Cook, the artist, or, more specifically, the artist I was hoping to become.

Yip was our first director but he didn't make it past the out-of-town tryouts. It must have been very difficult when Cheryl Crawford, the producer, said, "You're not directing your show anymore," but the truth is that I don't remember much about being directed by Yip. I was in a complete nervous fog most of the time, an absolute nervous wreck over my acting. Cheryl, one of the very few female producers on Broadway at the time, could be a very tough businesswoman, but she was wonderful to me. She would come round and ask, "Are you okay? Have you had any lunch? Can I send out for you?" She was very attentive and sweet. We got along very well, and at one point she mentioned the possibility of my auditioning for *Paint Your Wagon*, the upcoming Lerner and Loewe show about the California gold rush. That audition never happened and ultimately, Olga San Juan was cast in the role of Jennifer. I think Cheryl just liked the way I sang.

When it became clear out of town that Yip wasn't up to directing the show, the producers brought in Daniel Mann. His first order of business became trying to teach me how to act. Jerry Courtland, my leading man, had some experience, but it was clear that we both needed some help. I remember Danny taking the two of us down to the theater basement while we were in Philadelphia and explaining that even though we weren't the stars of the show per se, the whole musical did in fact hang on our storyline. It was important that we be up to the task, so he spent many long hours in that basement helping us with our scenes, and also teaching us some basic acting techniques. Not only were we learning to act, but we also had to learn to work the marionettes, and at one point I sang to a hand puppet!

The funny thing was that even with my inexperience and insecurities, and despite the convoluted plot and political overtones, *Flahooley* received warm notices during our tryouts in New Haven and Philadelphia. The songs were delightful, audiences loved us, and we all thought we were coming into town with a hit on our hands. Well, we weren't the first to be wrong on that account.

My mother came up for the opening on May 14, 1951, and was thrilled that I had made it to Broadway. My father flew in later, equally happy for me, but it's a visit that I remember chiefly because it was the only time my father said anything negative to me about my mother: "Nell is her own worst enemy." That's all he said. This was a big trip for my father, because he'd had a heart attack right after I moved to New York in 1948; although he recovered from that and could still work, he was never quite the same. But he wanted to see me in the show, and I remember the two of us having dinner at a steakhouse I used to go to with Herb Shriner. I felt grown up, but oh, I was so young and inexperienced. I felt I was living out a scenario from one of my favorite movies— young girl, determined to make it in New York, lands a big role in a brand-new Broadway musical. She's discovered and stars in a big smash hit. There was just one problem with that scenario: this wasn't a smash hit. Or a small hit. It was a complete flop.

I had actually been unsure of how the show would be received. I knew it was a strange show, but out-of-town audiences had liked it. Now, however, I was about to learn the lesson that there are always two different shows: the show that the audience sees and the show that you're in. When you're performing you are standing inside the show and there is no way to be objective. You can't judge the quality of the show because you're not seeing it. People talk to me about *Candide*, and I have to say, "I never saw *Candide*. I saw where I was but I never saw the show *Candide*."

When you're in a show you lose perspective. It's inevitable and happens as soon as you're immersed in rehearsals. I did a tiny bit of directing once and I was shocked at how quickly I lost perspective. I did see *The Music Man*, because I went to see it when I was on vacation from the show, and it was quite a revelation. When performing in the show I could never figure out why audiences loved the counterpoint of "Lida Rose/Will I Ever Tell You?" so much, but when I watched the show I really understood. Oh, that Buffalo Bills quartet that sang "Lida Rose" was terrific—a real barbershop quartet—and Meredith Willson's soaring melody for Marian (my character) on "Will I Ever Tell You?" provided the perfect contrast. Watching from the audience allowed me to see how genuinely crowd-pleasing the music and staging were.

Flahooley, however, was another matter entirely, because it didn't run long enough for me to ever take a day off and see the show. I remember standing in Times Square at midnight reading the opening-night review in the *New York Times*; Brooks Atkinson, the most influential of all critics at the time, called the show "a tedious antic with no humor or imagination at the heart of things," which seems a strange criticism for a show which in retrospect seemed to suffer from, if anything, *too much* imagination. Just to make sure no one missed his point, he added: "The plot is one of the most complicated, verbose and humorless of the season." Brooks Atkinson was a first-rate critic, someone who really cared about theater—he would follow people's careers and try to help them. He liked actors, which is not always the case with critics; but his review obviously spelled big trouble for us.

Some critics were charmed by the show's whimsy: John Chapman in the *Daily News* described it as "a tuneful, extraordinarily beautiful and delightfully imaginative musical." He also homed in on its political aspects, writing that "it may also be the most elaborately coated propaganda bill ever to be put on a stage."

Whether a propaganda bill or not, it wasn't onstage for very long. With the reviews skewing toward the negative, audiences in New York reacted much less enthusiastically to the show than they had out of town and we closed on June 16th, after just forty performances. We did record the cast album, and I received a tiny percentage for my work. And when I say tiny, I mean very, very tiny. This recording did not exactly sell like *My Fair Lady* would five years later. (The cast recording of *My Fair Lady* was an enormous top-of-the-charts hit, and once all that money was made—and paid out to the artists—record companies moved to make it much more difficult for performers to see any money from a cast recording. The record companies didn't want to share it with the people singing on the record, so subsequently we were simply paid a flat fee—usually one week's salary—with no provision for royalties on the album's future earnings.)

The closing of the show was terribly disappointing after the warm responses we'd had on the road. My first Broadway musical was now behind me, and the immediate future remained highly uncertain. When, later that year, I was singing at the Blue Angel, Orson Bean was also on the bill, and during a sound check he gave me a pep talk: "Oh, Barbara—it's great. You've got it made now. You've done a Broadway show and you don't have anything to worry about." Orson's a nice man, but was he ever wrong! It would be over two years before I landed another show.

In the meantime, however, it was June 1951 and I was heading back to Tamiment for my second summer. That second year in the Poconos would turn out to be a momentous one for me because it was there that I met David LeGrant, the man who would become my one and only husband, and a profound influence on my life in many ways. He was the only acting teacher I've ever studied with, a deeply talented man who for unknown reasons was unable to claim his place as a fine director.

Most important of all, he became the father of my darling son, Adam.

6 · MEETING DAVID LEGRANT

RETURNING TO TAMIMENT meant I could earn another five hundred dollars for the summer, so I didn't just think a return to Tamiment would be nice—I was eager. It meant money, fun, and a summer in the country. I never guessed I might acquire a husband along the way.

Prior to meeting David I'd had a few dalliances, but none of them was really serious. With David it was the real thing. We met in June of 1951, and while David was not a handsome man by conventional standards, I was drawn to his sensitivity, his superb talent, and a certain gentle quality in his personality. He seemed rooted. Solid. Looking back on it now, I think what attracted me most of all was that he seemed to have a lot of the "answers." He seemed very sure about the basic issues in life, and just a few weeks into our ten-week Tamiment season, we became inseparable. I don't remember when we started thinking and talking about the possibility of marriage, but by the time the summer had ended and we returned to the city, we thought we might get married.

There was one big problem, however. My mother. She had recently come to New York to live with me—in many ways it was inevitable that she would follow me to New York because I was her life. She was, however, dead set against my being with David, much less marrying him, and I think the prospect of our marriage may have been the deciding factor in her move to New York—she really wanted to stop us from marrying. In her view, David was poor as hell, wore tattered clothes, and had no real prospects. I knew about his talent, but even if my mother had been aware of that, it wouldn't have mattered to her. She just felt he was terrible husband material—he wasn't handsome, he was penniless, and, worst of all, in her mind, he was Jewish.

She did everything she could to stop us. At one point there was even a very dramatic scene in the kitchen when she picked up a knife and threatened him. Of course she wasn't really going to stab David, and she certainly was never physically violent to me when I was growing up, but when you look at photos from our wedding day you can see her anger; she made no attempt to hide her scowl.

I was in a terrible state. It wasn't just the ignorance of her prejudice—it's that it was so dumb on her part. If you want to have any kind of a relationship with a daughter whom you adore, then you sure as hell better find a way to get along with her partner or you're excluded, which is exactly what eventually happened. A lot of the time she was just excluded from our life together.

Her blatant anti-Semitism was just continuing a theme that had started all the way back when I was in high school. I was going out with a Jewish boy at the time, and when I'd leave the apartment she would ask: "You going out with the kike tonight?" I had a Chinese friend—same thing: "You goin' out with the chink tonight?" The casual use of those slurs was so upsetting to me. It bothered me enormously in high school and even more so when applied to the man I was going to marry.

Equally horrifying was the letter she wrote to David's mother, who was a really sweet, very naïve kind of peasant lady from Ekaterinoslav, in the Ukraine. Never having met her, my mother still wrote her a letter saying something like "Your lousy stinking Jew black-balled son wants to marry my gorgeous daughter"—and on and on. This poor lady didn't know how the hell to react. When you think about it, my mother's horrible letter to David's mother is a specimen of the following sort: you might be angry enough to write it, but you sure as hell don't mail it.

I liked David's mother very much, and I still have fond memories of driving cross-country to California to meet her for the first time. On that trip, David and I didn't even have money for restaurant food; we bought a big salami, which we could keep for some time, then a jar of mayonnaise, and a new loaf of bread every day. That was our daily ration, and we made that salami last through half of the United States!

One memory of that trip which is decidedly more embarrassing revolves around our stops at Native American reservations. I would go out of my way to demonstrate my friendliness—asking these Native Americans, who were total strangers, and whom I would never see again, how they were feeling and what their day was like. This behavior, understandably enough, embarrassed David, but I think the horrible racist attitudes I had encountered growing up simply pushed me too far in the opposite direction. Such inappropriate sentiment was my way of trying to say, "I'm not like the others." I still cringe thinking about it.

As I've gotten older and gained a little perspective I find myself believing that my mother was not well. The mechanism that keeps most people from acting on their most awful urges, such as writing that hateful letter to David's mother, was often simply missing in her.

I understand perfectly well how tricky it is to be a sidewalk psychiatrist, but for years it never occurred to me that my mother might be ill. In the past few years some friends have suggested she might have been bipolar. I tend to doubt that. I've shared stories about my mother's behavior with a friend who is a psychologist and she confirmed my hunch that my mother's problem was a borderline personality disorder.

Right at this time of our possible marriage, David and I were both cast in a tab show called *Six on a Honeymoon*, directed by our friend Herbert Ross. It would be a tour of five or six months, playing some of the better hotel rooms across the country, including the very prestigious Blackstone in Chicago. We decided that it made sense to set out on this tour as a married couple rather than as two besotted people who would have to sneak around to be together; in those days things were not as open and easy as they are now, and spending the night together could involve all sorts of machinations.

Deciding to get married was still not easy for me because I had lots of doubts, but I finally decided to take the step, and we were married—twice. We had wanted both Christian and Jewish ceremonies on the same day—that way we would have only one anniversary. The problem was that because the rules regarding marriage were so strict back in the early 1950s, we couldn't find a rabbi who would marry us, so we were first married in a Christian service. It was about a week after that ceremony, one conducted by a minister, when Eddie Harburg found a liberal rabbi who would marry us, and we happily arranged a little ceremony, which was held right in Eddie and Yip's Manhattan living room.

We married for that second time on Sunday March 2, 1952, while we were in rehearsal. We weren't children—I was twenty-four years old and David was twenty-eight—but I was completely unprepared to assume the responsibility of having another person's feelings in my hands. With my mother having taken the fortune-teller's advice about sparing me from any work completely to heart, I had grown up without performing even the most basic household duties—I simply had never had to pull my own weight. Without ever having had to wash dishes, cook a meal, or clean the house, I was ill prepared for life as someone's partner. I had a lot of growing up to do.

When we went back to rehearsal the day after our marriage, I remember going into the bathroom, looking in the mirror, suddenly sobbing, and saying out loud to myself that I had made a terrible mistake. I was not prepared to be a wife, and I broke down sobbing. I studied my tearstained face in the mirror and knew there was no way I was going to walk away from this marriage. I would stick with it and make it work. And it did work for a long time.

I came to love David very much. I came to depend deeply on him—ironically, so, too, did my mother—and he was an ideal husband in many ways. Very responsible. Never forgot to pick up the laundry. Never forgot to buy the loaf of bread. Would much rather be at home puttering around with me than running around with the guys or doing things on his own. Very, very dependable. We never stopped talking—we were both interested in the arts—theater, music, acting, and film. I was emotionally attracted to his talent and sensitivity. I didn't worry about his not yet making much money—I made money and felt confident that I would continue to do so. We were sympatico in many ways. And . . . I knew that David would never leave me the way my father had.

Shortly after we married, David gave me what I referred to as the The Sermon on the Mount. Looking me straight in the eye, he declared: "Follow me and everything will be okay. Let me lead you and you'll be fine the rest of your life." I believed that. I thought, "I don't have to worry about things because David knows what to do. I can just concentrate on my work. He's got it worked out." No surprise, then, that when I once said to a therapist that I'd married the wrong man, he instantly said to me: "You married the *right* one. Your neuroses dovetailed perfectly."

WHILE DAVID AND I were negotiating married life in the suburb of Port Washington, Long Island, I of course still harbored career ambitions. In 1951, *Flahooley* had been a fast flop, but I had attracted attention and eventually landed great roles in City Center productions of two Rodgers and Hammerstein musicals that were already considered classics: *Oklahoma!*, in which I played Ado Annie, and *Carousel*, in which I played Carrie Pipperidge. I had a terrific time with both roles: Ado Annie was the girl who "Cain't Say No," and Carrie sang the joy-filled "When I Marry Mr. Snow."

Under the leadership of Jean Dalrymple, City Center, on West Fifty-fifth Street in New York City, was producing limited runs of these musicals. In 1953–54 we did an entire season on the road with *Oklahoma!* but first we played the month of September at City Center in New York; I was Ado Annie and David played the peddler, Ali Hakim. We then went on the road and had a good time together. It was during that tour that I really got to know Florence Henderson, who was playing Laurey, and we have remained friends to this day. She is a genuinely talented and thoroughly nice woman, with a particular fondness for playing against her wholesome image by shocking others.

One problem during the tour of *Oklahoma!* was Mary Marlo, who played Aunt Eller and proved to be a genuine pain in the ass. She fancied herself quite the grande dame, and would make pronouncements like "You simply cannot entertain while on tour— you don't have the proper china and crystal." There was also a second fly in the ointment: Jerome Whyte, one of the casting directors for Rodgers and Hammerstein, who directed the tour. He insisted that I copy Celeste Holm, who had originated the role. Well, for any actor, that's death. It's just impossible. You have to discover the role for yourself. I was so unhappy trying to be Celeste that I began trying to make this my own Ado Annie. Jerry Whyte watched a performance, came backstage, and told me that if I continued to give my own interpretation he would see to it that I never worked again.

By way of contrast, when I was playing Carrie in *Carousel*, Dick Rodgers came to watch a rehearsal and noted that I did not get the laugh Jean Darling, the original Carrie, used to get with a funny piece of business with her bustle. I said to Dick, "Why would I walk that way at only this one point when I never walk that way again in the entire show. I can get the laugh another way without the business with the bustle." He listened and let me do it my own way.

I played Carrie Pipperidge from June to August of 1954. Bill Hammerstein, Oscar's son, directed *Carousel*, and there was no question but that it represented my best work thus far, a true breakthrough for me. With newfound confidence in my acting, I felt liberated onstage. For the first time I received major, major reviews, the general tone of which was: "This new person has happened!" I had been brought to the attention of the press and my face was everywhere. Suddenly I was being touted as the new theater discovery.

Both Richard Rodgers and Oscar Hammerstein came to see

me in *Carousel* and were very complimentary. Dick Rodgers was much more effusive than Oscar. Dick had an eye for the girls—well maybe it was both eyes for the girls—but he never chased me around. That may be because on the one day he asked me up to his office, I nervously opened the door to find that he had one foot gingerly positioned on a hassock; he had gout, so at least on that one day I knew I wouldn't be chased around his desk. I remember Oscar as being very tall with a warm smile—people admired him so. He possessed an aura of goodness—a very moral person. He didn't throw around a lot of compliments, but when he saw me in *The King and I* and said, "That's the best you've ever done," it meant the world.

It was also during this time that I screen-tested for the role of Ado Annie in director Fred Zinnemann's screen adaptation of *Oklahoma!* At the time of my screen test, Joanne Woodward and Paul Newman were up for the roles of Laurey and Curley, Eli Wallach was trying out for the role of Ali Hakim, and Rod Steiger was up for the role of Jud Frye. Rod was the only one from our group who was chosen to be in the film.

My clearest memory of that test involves standing right next to the director as he filmed Joanne Woodward doing Laurey's speech about wanting a cut-glass sugar bowl. I thought she was terrible—that she wasn't doing anything. When she finished, Zinnemann turned to me and said, "Now, there's a screen actress for you. She's going to have a big career in film." I was amazed, because standing just a few feet away I saw nothing happening, but he was certainly right.

I liked Fred Zinnemann very much and only wish we had worked together. I was disappointed to be turned down, but since

Shirley Jones was playing the role of Laurey, perhaps we were too much the same type for me to be in the film as Ado Annie. I had successfully played Ado Annie onstage but it's often the case that actors famous for their stage performances are not chosen for the film versions of those very same shows. Carol Channing was passed over in favor of Barbra Streisand for the film version of *Hello, Dolly!* Julie Andrews lost the chance to play Eliza Doolittle in the movie of *My Fair Lady* when the producers and director chose Audrey Hepburn. And perhaps most famously, Ethel Merman never filmed *Gypsy*. Rosalind Russell, who played the role of Rose in the movie, is a wonderful actress, but Ethel Merman *was* Rose. If only her performance had been preserved forever on film.

In 1954, I also appeared in a television soap opera called *Golden Windows*, playing an aspiring singer who sang off-key. It was filmed live in New York City but didn't last long. For the most part I enjoyed the experience; it is very rewarding to know that you are reaching millions of people at the same time, but the frantic nature of live TV was very stressful. There was no second chance once those cameras rolled—you better pay attention and get it right the first time, because there ain't no second time!

By this point I was also studying voice, although my lessons had come about in a rather unusual way. In 1953 it was actually my husband who started lessons with Bob Kobin, the man who would become my main voice teacher. At the beginning, I was so cautious that I wouldn't work with Bob. I would go with David to his lessons and just listen. This was partially in reaction to the fact that I had already endured two false starts with voice teachers; my first teacher was really more of a coach, a woman with whom I never really clicked, but she did help me with presentation. I remember that for some strange reason I would wear short gloves during lessons because they made me feel strong. Well, as Wally Harper used to say, "Whatever blows your skirt up."

After a second mismatch with a vocal coach, I was still hesitant, but I liked what I heard when Bob was teaching David, and I finally told him that I'd like to study with him. Bob based his entire technique on physiology, a very commonsense approach. We know how sound is produced—it's not a big mystery—but many teachers don't take that into account. Bob's techniques, however, had a sound basis in science. Now, I know this will sound crazy, but here's the story his wife, Joan, told me. Bob went to the slaughterhouse, collected a few cow larynxes, and dissected them, because they are, I'm told, so similar to human larynxes. He really wanted to know how the damn things actually worked.

Armed with this knowledge of physiology, Bob developed a theory that said that you, the singer, already know how to sing, but that you must, in effect, get out of your own way. Your body instinctively knows what is required, and if you are singing properly, every note you sing should strengthen your voice. In Bob's mind, you should be able to sing for a long time and not only not hurt yourself, but actually get better and stronger. He didn't want to hear about hot tea and lemon, scarves, drafts, or any of "that stuff." He used to tell me I should be able to get hit by a bus and then stand up and sing! Bob really helped me put my voice together in a way that didn't make me sound like I had four different voices. He would say, "This note needs to come out of the preceding one organically—it's as if you are making a string of pearls, so it needs to be continuous, logical, and organic."

My singing improved, and after my success in playing Carrie in *Carousel*, my confidence grew. I knew I could really sing, and I now began to feel that I could definitely act as well, that

I was capable of creating a flesh-and-blood character onstage and bringing the audience along on the journey with me.

So it was that in 1954, shortly before I was cast in *Plain and Fancy*, I went through a period of repeated auditions for *Peter Pan*. I literally auditioned at least ten times but Jerome Robbins, the director, couldn't decide between Kathy Nolan and me. Regardless of Jerry's reputation for being mean, he was always very kind to me and clearly seemed to respect my talent, even though the role eventually went to Kathy. Because she sat in on all of these auditions, Mary Martin began to take a real interest in me and my career. Even though I didn't get the job, she would send me little gifts—it was so nice of her. She was the biggest star on Broadway and it was all very flattering. *Peter Pan* played at the Winter Garden, and when we later went into that same theater with *Plain and Fancy*, she, knowing which dressing room I was going to be in, had written on the mirror in lipstick: "Good luck from Peter Pan. Peter loves you."

Well, a few years later my mother was visiting me after a performance of *Candide* and was in my dressing room when up the stairs came Mary Martin and her husband, Richard Halliday. I saw them coming and I froze: I could not remember Richard Halliday's name to save my life. I knew I had to introduce them to my mother, so I decided to be honest and say to him, "I'm sorry. I don't know how this could have happened but your name has just flown out of my head. I apologize." Mary never spoke to me again.

I may not have won the role in *Peter Pan*, but my confidence continued to grow; when I auditioned for *Plain and Fancy*, far from perspiring throughout the audition, I walked onto that stage feeling like I could do no wrong. I knew in my bones that I could do this. I remember singing "Mr. Snow" for Franz Allers, the conductor, and I was then asked to read a scene; when the creative team learned that I had never seen that particular scene before, they were so happy with my first attempt that the role was mine.

I was to play a naïve Amish girl, Hilda Miller, who has lived her entire life in an Amish community without ever once venturing to a city. She runs away and has adventures, all to the accompaniment of a very entertaining score by Albert Hague and Arnold Horwitt. We had a great cast, including Nancy Andrews, Richard Derr, and Shirl Conway (the unknown Bea Arthur was Shirl's standby). I thought the show could be a lot of fun, and I was right; this was a musical that seemed to work well right from the beginning.

Even rehearsals were great, including a cast field trip that proved just how interesting this business can be. Part of the action in *Plain and Fancy* involved the full company singing "How Do You Raise a Barn?" as we gathered to build a new barn, so we all went to the Feller Scenery Shop in the Bronx, where they were building the set, in order to gain hands-on experience with the onstage barn. By hands-on, I mean literally hands-on, because we all learned to simulate a real barn raising—where to put our hands, how to hoist the planks, and how to work together just as Amish farmers would. The first time we tried to raise the stage barn, it took twenty minutes, which obviously would never do. We did it over and over, cutting down the number of minutes it took, until we finally made it within the allotted amount of time. It was so exciting that it was like winning the Derby! Audiences loved that moment in the show, but nothing ever quite touched that wonderful feeling of family togetherness we experienced in the scene shop.

Audiences liked *Plain and Fancy* from the start of our out-of-town tryout, although I had a humorous (in retrospect) moment with my song "I'll Show Him." That particular song, which I was to sing right before running off to the carnival, had not been written as a typical soprano solo, and as a result necessitated my singing in a different style than usual. I was worried about the song and went to our director, Morton "Tec" Da Costa, and our choreographer, Helen Tamiris, to explain my solution: "I want to cut one of my songs." Needless to say, they had never before heard those words from an up-and-coming actress, and simply looked at me before bursting out in laughter. That was the end of the discussion.

We opened in January of 1955 at the Mark Hellinger Theatre, quickly switched to the Winter Garden for the rest of the year, and then returned to the Hellinger for the final four months of the run, closing in March of 1956, after 461 performances. I received some great notices, and when I recently looked up some of those reviews I was actually a bit startled at how enthusiastic the big critics really were. Walter Kerr, then at the *New York Herald Tribune*, wrote: "Barbara Cook, right off a blue and white Dutch plate, is delicious all the time, but especially when she perches on a trunk, savors her first worthwhile kiss, and melts into the melody of 'This Is All Very New to Me.'"

Something about the spirit of the show—the real sense of community it conveyed—seemed to touch people deeply. During our run, a woman who had left the Amish community wrote me; she had loved the show and sent me a few of her old Amish caps, including a very special dress-up one. I still have those caps.

It was during *Plain and Fancy* that I appeared in a network television production of *Babes in Toyland*. The surprising thing is that I don't have strong memories of the production, even though there were major television personalities involved; the show was produced by Max Liebman, one of the leading TV producers of the time, and my costars included Wally Cox, Dennis Day, Dave Garroway (of *The Today Show* fame), and the Bil and Cora Baird marionettes (the Bairds gained worldwide fame for their work on the film version of *The Sound of Music*).

I actually have stronger memories of my February 1956 appearance in a television production of *Bloomer Girl*, but not for the right reasons. The director, Alex Segal, was difficult and for unfathomable reasons chose to make life miserable for the terrific character actor Paul Ford, who was playing my father. The length of the show had to be cut to fit the TV time format, and for some reason Segal chose to cut every scene where I was wearing bloomers. And the title of the show was . . . ?

We had terrific choreography by Agnes de Mille, and I enjoyed singing that beautiful Harold Arlen/Yip Harburg score, including "Right as the Rain," but when I saw a tape of the show recently at the New York Paley Center for Media I found it nothing so much as embarrassing. There I was in my Shirley Temple curls, turning in a less-than-award-winning acting performance.

Plain and Fancy was a good experience for me, but when I remember that time I always find myself thinking about the difficult political climate. Stefan Schnabel, a wonderful character actor, played my uncle, and one day when I mentioned that I was going to an Actors' Equity meeting, he advised me that I would be better off not going. He said people would be writing down everything that was said, taking notes on any suspicious Communist-sounding talk, so I didn't attend. Given my liberal leanings, I now think that if I had been older and less naïve I probably would have been blacklisted. Senator Joe McCarthy had only been censured by the Senate one month before we opened. President Eisenhower had not even spoken out against the accusations McCarthy lodged against his friend General George Marshall, until he deemed it safe to do so. When I think about the fact that General Marshall devised "the Marshall Plan" to help feed starving people in Europe after the war, yet was accused of Communist sympathies, it boggles my mind. It was a tough, tough time in this country.

8 · LEONARD BERNSTEIN
AND *CANDIDE*

I HAD A good time in *Plain and Fancy*, and it was icing on the cake when I received a Theatre World Award for my performance. After the show closed on Broadway I did a summer-stock production of the show in Pittsburgh, in which Elaine Stritch played Ruth, the Shirl Conway role. I had also performed the show with Bea Arthur when she went on for Shirl in New York, and even then both Elaine and Bea were formidable women. Bea's performance, although wonderful, was so different from Shirl's that it threw me, because I didn't yet have the acting experience to deal with such a big change onstage. I was also offered the London production of the show at the Drury Lane Theatre, but I decided against that because I would have had to stay with the London company for at least six months, which I felt was too long a time to be away from David.

So, future unknown, I auditioned for Frank Loesser's *The Most Happy Fella*. Oh, I wanted to do that show so badly. It's such a beautiful score: "Somebody Somewhere," "Warm All Over"— those songs are as good as it gets. But, disappointed as I was not to land the show, if I had I would not have been free to take on my next musical. As is so often the case, it all started out very innocently . . .

Just as *Plain and Fancy* was winding down its run in 1956, the phone rang very early one morning. David answered and passed the phone over to me. It was Ethel Reiner, one of the producers of a new show called *Candide*. I had vaguely heard about it—it was going to be some kind of opera/operetta/musical written by Leonard Bernstein and Lillian Hellman. I hadn't paid much attention because I felt certain that it was not something I would be considered for, so I was surprised to get the call. Ethel wanted to know if I could sing a high C. I told her yes, though I didn't add that I had never sung a high C, or any other note even remotely that high, in public. That little G right over the top of the staff was it, as far as my public performances were concerned.

Now, this is where my training with Bob Kobin came in very handy. Bob always insisted that all his students had to learn arias, no matter what kind of music they intended to sing. I resisted like crazy: "Why do I have to learn this stuff. I'm not gonna be an opera singer. All that *ah-ah-aaaaaah* stuff is too hard. I don't want to do it." He persisted, however, and finally he played an aria that I thought was so beautiful I was willing to give it a try.

The first aria I worked on was "*Non mi dir*" from Mozart's *Don Giovanni*. Not right for my voice in the least, but he was happy that I was willing to try something, no matter how ill suited. I went on to learn arias by Puccini, Verdi—all the greats—never thinking that they might be useful one day. In the process of these lessons I learned that I had all these high notes I hadn't even known about. I didn't really take it seriously. To me it was like I was pretending to be an opera singer. I could hit a high C, sure. But I wasn't going to be singing at the Met. Little did I know . . .

At any rate, Ethel and I made a date for me to come in and sing, but on the appointed day I had a bad stomach virus and had to cancel. I didn't hear anything back from her for a couple of months, and I just forgot about it. Then, out of the blue, she called back and we made another date. This time I was going to sing for Leonard Bernstein, who had written the score. By then he was already a well-known conductor, had written film scores, several Broadway shows, and quite a few very impressive classical pieces. He was already LEONARD BERNSTEIN, so I was, as usual, nervous as hell.

When I arrived on time at Ms. Reiner's office the maestro had yet to appear, so she said, "While you're waiting, perhaps you'd like to take a look at this aria written for the role of Cunegonde." This was the first time I heard the name of the role I was up for, and also the first time I saw the music for "Glitter and Be Gay." It was twelve pages long. Holy Hannah!

I looked at the music and saw all those lines above the staff. I didn't, and don't, read music but I sure as hell knew what all those extra lines above the treble clef meant. In other words, this was a killer piece of music and certainly something I would never be hired to do. (During rehearsals I counted the high notes in the score for Cunegonde—four E-flats above high C, six D-flats above high C, sixteen B-flats, and twenty-one high C's.) Funny thing, it seemed so out of reach that instead of making me more nervous, looking at the music calmed me down, because I felt certain that I would never be hired to sing this thing. I thought, "Okay, I get to meet Leonard Bernstein, it's a nice day, I'll sing, go home, and have a nice life."

Suddenly—pow! Leonard Bernstein swept into the room, and when I say swept I aint kiddin'. He was wearing a rather long, green, loden cape lined in red satin that swirled around him, an outfit finished off by black patent-leather loafers. Wow!

Sam Krachmalnick, the man who was to conduct the show, arrived with the maestro. We went into a small room with a piano and I sang the song I usually auditioned with, Arthur Schwartz and Dorothy Fields's "Make the Man Love Me" from *A Tree Grows in Brooklyn*. When I finished, the maestro looked at me and said, "Very nice—what else do you have?" Because I knew they wanted to hear my high notes, I told him I planned to sing "You Are Love," complete with a high C ending. He very quickly said, "Don't sing 'You Are Love.' I know exactly how you'd sing 'You Are Love.'"

That hit me hard. I hadn't planned anything else. I knew I had to come up with something else, but what? Twenty seconds passed—three years in audition time. Then an idea popped into my head—what about all those arias Bob had insisted on my learning? And then before I knew what I was doing, I found myself saying to LEONARD BERNSTEIN, "I guess I could sing Madame Butterfly's entrance music for you, but I don't have the music." "That's okay," he said, "I know it." At which point he sat down at the piano . . . omigod!

I started the aria just as Bob had taught me, but Bernstein was in a different place. Finally we realized that for some reason Bob hadn't taught me the very beginning of the aria, when Butterfly sings off-stage as she's climbing up the little hill to her house. I was starting at the point when she actually appears onstage for the first time.

We worked all that out and I sang that gorgeous Puccini music. Puccini wrote a high alternate ending for the aria that many people don't sing, but I thought, what the hell, if ever there was a time to try that high note this was it. So . . . I sang the bejeezus out of that high D-flat. Bernstein was thrilled. I was shocked that I had actually done it. I'd never sung this music outside of my teacher's studio. Mr. Bernstein said, "You have great musical courage." I said, "You mean I got a lotta guts." He asked where I had gone to school, and I was so naïve that I almost answered "Girl's High." Thank God at the last instant I realized he meant music school, and I explained that I had no formal training of that sort. It was decided that I would have a few sessions with Sam to work on "Glitter and Be Gay" so we could all see if I could really sing this thing.

I also began working again with Bob Kobin, who was great, as always. When we started to really examine the piece, he looked at me and said, "Of course you can do this. You have that high E-flat. Don't worry about it."

During one of my sessions with Sam Krachmalnick, he mentioned to me, as if in passing, "Lenny's going to come by today to see how we're doing." By this time I could sing the piece all the way through, and although he didn't tell me, I should have known that Bernstein would make his mind up that day whether it made sense to continue with me or not.

I sang for Bernstein, and it went well, but passing that preliminary test is not what I remember most clearly from that day. Instead, it's that I suggested to LEONARD BERNSTEIN what I thought would prove to be a better way to end one of his musical phrases. Amazing! How did I ever have the nerve to say such a thing? Well, it just seemed obvious to me, and, even more surprisingly, Bernstein agreed with me and changed the phrase.

Here's the phrase in question:

> *Born to higher things,*
> *Here I droop my wings . . .*
> *Aaaaaaaaaaaaaah*

That "aaaaah" is a high C. Very hard for me to sing and cut off cleanly, as it was written. So—I suggested doing a portamento down from the high C to a lower note at the end of the "aaaaaah." It made perfect sense to me. Cunegonde was talking about drooping her wings, so why not "droop" the note?

When I think about this scenario now, I shake my head in disbelief at the confidence I had. I suppose a better word to describe my action would be "clueless." This was only the second time I had been in the same room with the composer, and this was not just any composer. This was Maestro Leonard Bernstein. I'd never sung this kind of song in public. I was a musical-comedy actress with a mere two Broadway shows under my belt, and I was now telling this genius how to improve his aria? It was like rehearsing *Flahooley* and telling the conductor that I wasn't going to change my singing—they'd have to change the orchestration. Where the hell I got that chutzpah from I have absolutely no idea.

I suggested the change, and Bernstein smiled and said, "You're absolutely right. Why didn't I think of that?" It was a portent of things to come: from the start of rehearsals through to closing night, Lenny made me feel that I could do anything.

I had passed this preliminary test with Bernstein, but as auditions continued I was asked to come to the Mark Hellinger Theatre to not only sing again for the maestro, but also to meet Lillian Hellman, who was writing the book for the show.

I admired Lillian greatly. During the time of Senator McCarthy's terrible witch hunt for Communists, when the House Un-American Activities Committee was doing its dreadful work, everyone lived in fear, and careers were lost. Lillian, however, was not cowed. One of the reasons she suggested *Candide* to Lenny as a possible musical piece was because there is a scene in Voltaire's original—an auto-da-fé in Lisbon—which was very reminiscent of what was happening in our country. All the name-calling. All

the accusations. Friend against friend. *Candide* provided these artists with a means of standing tall and publicly showing their disap-
proval of McCarthyism and HUAC.

That very first afternoon at the Mark Hellinger, Lillian asked
me: "Do you think you can play a young European girl?" At
that point in my life I had been to Niagara Falls and Tijuana, end
of story, but of course I said yes. I wasn't going to lose this role,
dammit, even though I didn't know if I really could play a European.

That same afternoon in the theater, Bernstein had me sing
phrases in 5/4 time, then in 7/4 time, really pushing me. Three
days later I was told the role was mine.

Fortunately there were still several weeks before rehearsals officially began, which gave me a lot of time to learn the score. Bob
Kobin helped me find an opera coach—Wolfgang (can't remember
his last name)—a wonderful man who taught me a lot. I worked
with him on all of the music and learned a great deal of plain old
technical musical know-how.

I had great teachers, no question, but as rehearsals began, I was
beside myself with fear. Holy shit! I had one thought: What have I
agreed to do? If I messed up it wasn't like the mistake wouldn't be
noticed—this was Leonard Bernstein and Lillian Hellman. The
public was going to pay attention.

I talked about my fears constantly to anybody I came across, an
action that infuriated David. He felt that if he told me I could do it,
then his reassurance ought to be all I needed to hear. I didn't mean
to upset him, but when I'm concerned about something I need to
air it, again and again. I couldn't help talking about my fear, because in the very beginning I couldn't even finish "Glitter and Be
Gay." Literally.

The muscles just wouldn't do it. It was like trying to carry heavy groceries home and coming to that moment when you just have to set them down. The muscles just give out and you have to rest. The same thing is true for the voice, and with "Glitter and Be Gay" I couldn't cross the finish line. So—I had Wolfgang record the accompaniment for me and every day when I came home from rehearsal, before I started to relax too much, I would sing through the aria twice without stopping. It was just like training for a sporting event.

We had a fine cast and a famous English director, Tyrone Guthrie. The costumes were designed by Irene Sharaff, and the set by Oliver Smith. These were the premiere designers in all of theater, and Irene always insisted on the absolute best in our costumes. In the "I Am Easily Assimilated" number, the men wore very beautiful Spanish costumes—made in Spain, of course. I once asked her about a slip under one of my dresses which had a ten-inch border of handmade French lace. "Why this expensive lace, Irene? Nobody will see it." Irene simply stated: "But you will know it's there."

I loved working with Irene, and she's the only designer I worked with in all those years who gave me a beautiful watercolor sketch of one of my costumes. It was a sketch she knew I would treasure forever, that of the gorgeous dress I wore for "Glitter and Be Gay."

The lyrics to *Candide* were written by so many different people: Lillian wrote the beautiful words for "El Dorado." John Latouche and Dorothy Parker contributed as well, and I believe that Ms. Parker wrote many, if not all of the words for "Glitter and Be Gay." Lenny supplied the words for the contralto Irra Petina's big number, "I Am Easily Assimilated"; in that song he wrote the lyric "My father came from Rovna Gubernya," utilizing that strange name because his father had been born in Rovna Gubernya. The poet Richard Wilbur wrote several lyrics, including our beautiful finale, "Make Our Garden Grow." Imagine five different lyricists, all of them incredibly talented in their fields. Well, there never was another show like it.

All of us in the cast knew it was a one-of-a-kind show, and while we didn't have big discussions about the show's political resonance, we were all quite aware of it. The creators were trying to make a statement without losing sight of the entertainment value, and all of their ideas were floating around Bernstein's score. This show felt entirely different and new. It was exciting to be around the day-to-day process, and my lack of formal musical training didn't faze Lenny in the least. One day in the midst of the constant craziness that is part of rehearsing a big musical, he asked me: "Can you trill?" I said, "No, but I can fake it." He laughed. "Go ahead and try. Everybody fakes it anyway."

Our Candide was Robert Rounseville, who was perfectly cast. He was difficult, but not intentionally so. He was just kind of absentminded. I was often barefoot in the show, and he'd be kneeling down next to me onstage, and sometimes he would kneel right on my toes. Let me tell you—when somebody puts all their weight on your toes it hurts like hell. I'd say, "Bob, please be careful." And then he'd do it again—he didn't mean to, he was just in another world. I think he had a little drinking problem, too, but he sang like an angel.

The "Governor," William Olvis, had a beautiful baritone voice, although he was a little nuts, but the capper was Irra Petina who played "The Old Lady." She was the embodiment of every bad joke you've ever heard about an opera diva. She was absolutely paranoid—convinced I was trying to steal every moment from her. If I came up with a piece of business, she would repeat it right after me. When we all lined up for our final bows, she always, and I mean always, put her hand in front of my face. I had my little ivory fan with me, and when I gently whacked her hand she always looked surprised, as if she had no idea what she had done. A few days before we opened on Broadway, Tyrone Guthrie called a rehearsal and gave us all notes. We were sitting in a circle on the stage. Irra happened to be next to me, and Dr. Guthrie spoke to me first. He said, "Barbara, what you're doing is fine—it just needs to be bigger. You need to make bigger gestures." Then he said to Irra: "The opposite is true for you. I need for you to tone it down." Irra looked at Tyrone Guthrie and immediately replied: "Well, if Barbara would do it bigger, then my performance wouldn't look so big."

The stage manager had it even worse with Irra. When he went to her dressing room to give her a performance note she smacked him! What a piece of work she was. When I look back on her behavior now, it seems laughable, but at the time I found her to be a complete pain in the ass.

Most of the cast, with the exception of the character actors and Max Adrian, our "Dr. Pangloss," were all opera singers. It was very intimidating, not only for me but also for Max. He was upset because he had told Bernstein the absolute limits of his vocal range and then Lenny had written beyond it in the "Gavotte." As a result, Max was struggling with the number and was a bit miffed, but he also happened to be an island of common sense. My favorite gem of his: "When in rehearsal never stand if you can sit, and never sit if you can lie down." Oh, what a nice man Max was.

We began rehearsals and I'd continually find myself looking around the room at Leonard Bernstein, Lillian Hellman, Tyrone Guthrie, Irene Sharaff, Richard Wilbur, and—who? *Me? Barbara Cook?* That's not false modesty. It's really how I felt then.

As rehearsals progressed, every time we got to the place where I should be singing "Glitter," they skipped over it, to save my voice, I suppose. They may have been trying to save my voice, but it was also not helping me at all. My fear grew. The company had all heard of this difficult aria written for Cunegonde and certainly were aware of the fact that I was not an opera singer. Barbara Cook, Miss Musical Comedy of 1956, was going to sing this showpiece, so they were all very curious about the aria.

Again and again at rehearsal we would skip over the song until finally, knowing that I would eventually have to sing it in front of the entire company, I hatched a plan with one of the rehearsal pianists. I explained the situation to him and suggested that one day, as the cast straggled back from lunch, I would be singing the aria, pretending to have come back early so I could rehearse with the pianist. The plan worked. When the cast listened, they were excited for me. I had made it through! I wanted and needed my fellow cast members' approval, and when the song went over, I gained a little bit of confidence.

We went to Boston for our out-of-town tryouts, and I have a distinct memory of Lillian from that time, and of her extraordinary wardrobe. She was such a lady, and possessed great style; when we boarded the train for Boston she arrived with a dozen hatboxes and two huge wardrobe trunks.

We arrived in Boston and I was a wreck, but even so, we all had a hilarious moment on the night of the first preview. It was some sort of benefit and Guthrie went out to address the audience before we started: "The lighting may not all be focused. . . . Some of the actors don't have all of their costumes, and the scenery that is here may not work as it should—so just keep your peckers up." He was so British and of course that phrase does not mean quite the same there as it does here in the U.S. We were listening to him behind the curtain and we screamed with laughter. The fact that we were in "proper" Boston made it even funnier!

But that light moment didn't last. The night of that first preview, and at each succeeding performance, I'd hear the first few notes from the oboe at the start of "Glitter and Be Gay" and I would just freeze, frightened to death. I could only plant my feet, clasp my hands together, and pray I could get through the song one more time. The emotional fear was much more draining than any physical exertion—I couldn't work past the feeling that I was going to fall off the cliff. I was so miserable that I was seriously contemplating trying to leave the show—leaving a Leonard Bernstein musical when all I had wanted for most of my life was to be in Broadway musicals. I was one scared and confused young woman, and the creators knew I wasn't delivering properly. I was not having any fun, not acting it at all. I was still on the page, not on the stage. I didn't know what the hell to do, and it got to the point where I hated the idea of going to the theater, hated facing the terror that awaited me every night. An emotional impasse had developed, a barrier between me and the music. I was singing it but not feeling it at all.

And then . . . On matinee days I would have an early dinner by myself so I wouldn't have to talk, after which I would go back to my room to have a brief nap before the evening performance. On one of those afternoons I happened to pick up a copy of *Pageant* magazine so I could read while I ate, and inside I found an article about experiments with self-hypnosis that were being conducted at Duke University. As I read the article I began to wonder if self-hypnosis could help me with "Glitter and Be Gay." I decided that instead of napping in my room between shows, I would spend that time attempting to hypnotize myself. I relaxed, and, just as the magazine suggested, began to ease myself into a hypnotic state. I immediately knew that it was working. I felt very sure that I was in a suggestible state, so I told myself that when I "woke" I would feel a great surge of energy, and that I would be excited to arrive at the theater. I told myself "The moment you touch the stage door you will feel terrific energy and a great desire to sing the aria. With every application of makeup you will be filled with energy and a desire to be onstage singing 'Glitter and Be Gay.'" I was convinced this was going to work and that I would finally enjoy my potentially show-stopping moment.

And I did! And oh, how I enjoyed it. After the performance, the "brass" came rushing backstage to congratulate me. I had made the breakthrough! Maybe it was pure desperation that made it work, but it worked. Even though I had used the self-hypnosis in order to gain the extra energy, I never again needed it to help me sing that devilish aria. I tried to utilize the hypnosis for other areas of my life, but it never worked quite as well as it did that first time.

Thomas Pyle, who played multiple roles in the show, used to stand in the wings every night to time my applause. It was, well . . . spectacular! Sometimes it would last two or even three minutes. One night he swears it was four minutes—an eon in a show! I don't believe that it lasted four minutes, but I think the response was enormous for a combination of reasons: it's a great piece, I sang it well, and it was completely unexpected from this musical-comedy singer Barbara Cook. People felt "in" on this discovery, and audiences love the thrill of discovery. By now of course, I had come to love the song and my big moment.

Because *Candide* was such a demanding score, my doctor suggested I have complete vocal rest from the end of the Saturday-night show until the next performance on Monday evening. In theory I'd be resting my voice for a full forty-eight hours, but of course I'd forget to keep silent, and so I put a tiny Band-Aid over the corner of my mouth as a reminder not to speak! It worked.

The response to "Glitter and Be Gay" was thrilling, but, even with the big ovation, it was clear that the show had problems. The audience was often confused by what was happening onstage. Dr. Guthrie was a highly respected director, one whom Sir Peter Hall later termed "A towering figure, a brilliant and at times great director." Indeed, when it came to classical theater, I concurred; one of the best and funniest plays I've ever seen was his production of *Troilus and Cressida* (there was a five-minute comic section about heel-clicking and saluting that I will never forget!). But—and it's a big "but"—even with all of that talent, I think he was probably not the right person to direct *Candide*.

Lillian and the producers seemed to feel the same way, because when we came back to New York, Lillian herself took over rehearsals for a couple of days. I can't imagine what the meetings were like that led to her assuming the role of director, but I will say that our creative team were complete professionals—we never heard even one word of dissension among them.

My take on being directed by Tony Guthrie was that while he cared very much about production values and the overall concept, he was not particularly interested in helping the cast with whatever acting problems they might have been facing. I think he expected you to have all of those issues solved, because he had other, more important, matters to consider. I learned this firsthand when we were still out of town and I asked him for help with a new scene.

"Have you read it, my dear?"

"Dr. Guthrie—the scene has been in the show for a week now, so, yes, I've read it. I just don't fully understand it."

"Well, read it again, dahling."

As a result I worked out my approach to "Glitter and Be Gay" myself. When I was a teenager in Atlanta I had somehow acquired a 78 rpm recording of Orson Welles and Fay Bainter performing *Macbeth*, and I used to perform the "Out, damn spot" speech just for myself. Nobody was at home and I'd emote up a storm. "Out, I say! . . . Yet who would have thought the old man to have had so much blood in him?" It wasn't until some time after *Candide* closed that I realized I had based the "Glitter and Be Gay" dialogue on Fay Bainter. It was real, yet highly emotive.

I have two distinct memories of opening night in New York, December 1, 1956, at the Martin Beck Theatre. The first is that the overture stopped the show—people loved it, and to this day it's one of the most frequently played pieces by symphony orchestras around the world. In 1975, when I did my first big concert at Carnegie Hall, it occurred to me that, for sure, someone was going to ask me to sing "Glitter and Be Gay." Well, there's no way I was going to do that. But what I did do was pull out my kazoo and perform the beginning of the overture—on that kazoo!

My second big memory from opening night was Lenny coming backstage to wish me luck. He was just about to leave when he added, "Oh yes, Maria Callas is out front." If there was anything I didn't need to hear, it was those seven words. I said, "Oh my God, I could have done without knowing that." Lenny laughed and said, "Don't be ridiculous. She'd kill for your E-flats." Callas did not come backstage, and I'm sorry to say that, much as I would have liked to meet her, I never did. I would love to know what she thought about the show, and me, and "Glitter and Be Gay."

Oddly enough, for such a high-profile show, there was no big opening-night party. I went to the Plaza to have a little supper with my husband, Bob Kobin, and his wife, Joan. The reviews came out and, like the show itself, they were all over the place. We did receive some terrific reviews—John Chapman called it "the greatest addition to musical literature since *Rosenkavalier*"—but a great many critics called it confusing and overly ambitious. Walter Kerr in the *Herald Tribune* was the most damning of all. His opening paragraph ran as follows: "Three of the most talented people our theater possesses—Lillian Hellman, Leonard Bernstein and Tyrone Guthrie—have joined hands to transform Voltaire's *Candide* into a really spectacular disaster."

I never got to see our production from out front, so I couldn't objectively judge exactly what didn't work and why. I do know that audiences would leave the theater wondering what they had just seen. Was it a musical comedy? Not really. Was it an opera? No. It was unique, and in this case "unique" did not sell tickets.

The show lasted only seventy-three performances, closing on February 2, 1957, although later that spring the show was nominated for five Tony Awards, including Best Musical. Everyone blamed Lillian's book, and certainly there were major faults with it, but it's also just a problematic show. I've never seen a production of *Candide* that I thought worked. I think some of the problem lies in the fact that you just don't care about these people and their exotic misadventures.

But—*Candide* did great things for my career and I am extremely proud to have been a part of it. More than any other show in my career, *Candide* has given me a certain musical credibility I wouldn't have acquired otherwise, especially within the classical world. People who knew my work pre-*Candide* were, to say the least, surprised by this new "classical" Barbara. Franz Allers, the conductor with whom I worked on *Plain and Fancy*, was stunned and often spoke to me about the show throughout the ensuing years.

Candide has now had two Broadway revivals, most notably the first one, in 1974, directed by Hal Prince. It was an environmental production where they took all the seats out of the orchestra floor and replaced them with benches and cushions, an odd and cramped seating configuration; when Katharine Hepburn went to see the show with her *Lion in Winter* director Tony Harvey, she was so uncomfortable on her stool, that after deciding the actors onstage looked much more comfortable than anyone in the audience, she turned to Harvey and said to him: "Dare me to join them onstage?" He did, and she did.

But brilliant as Hal is, he made a very strange choice in that production. At the end of the show, the entire cast sings the absolutely gorgeous "Make Our Garden Grow," which was written while we were in rehearsal. Wilbur wrote the lyric first and Bernstein then went home to compose that beautiful melody. It's a transcendent, even spiritual moment, but while the cast was singing that extraordinary song, Hal had the cow come onstage and die at their feet. I just can't figure that one out.

That said, I must add that he is one of the most talented directors I've ever worked with. Yet here's another choice Hal made in *Candide* that strikes me as passing strange. In "Glitter and Be Gay" the singer takes center stage, but over on the left Hal had some person playing a pipe organ; the jewels, which are so important to the song, remained over by the pipe organ instead of being handy for Cunegonde. It was like the song was being performed by two different people—Cunegonde and the lady on the pipe organ. Frankly, all you have to do is stand there and inhabit the song.

Candide has lived on in our original cast recording, which I think is a good one. I remember singing all day during that recording session: there were trios, duets, and quartets that all featured Cunegonde, and we recorded those *before* I sang "Glitter and Be Gay," which was scheduled for after the dinner break. In other words, instead of just singing sporadically during a two-and-one-half-hour performance, I was scheduled to sing full out on multiple takes from eleven a.m. to five p.m., and then beyond. Knowing this could spell trouble for my voice, I forgot about dinner and went right to my doctor's office, where for the only time in my life I had my vocal cords shrunk with a spray. The doctor said they looked like a picket fence, they were so swollen from singing for so many hours. The spraying of vocal cords is a tricky procedure for a singer, but I trusted him, and it worked. (I've also never done it again.) I then went back to the recording studio and did three takes of the aria.

The funny thing is that Lenny couldn't be in the studio for the cast recording because he had a concert somewhere in the Caribbean. He showed up about eight p.m. and listened to some of the songs. He said Sam's tempos had been too fast. Maybe—but I think most people perform "Glitter and Be Gay" too slowly. Our recording is exciting as hell. To this day I receive compliments on "Glitter and Be Gay," and I repeatedly hear that no one has ever bettered my rendition. But—

The truth is that I hear lots of things wrong with my version. I think the main mistake most people make with this aria is thinking that they have to "make it funny." It is intrinsically funny and best when presented in earnest, as if sung by a dramatic teenager. It has to be carefully sung, particularly the "ha, ha, ha"s, because Bernstein did not intend them to be "runs." Each "ha" should be sung separately so that they sound like laughter. Lenny also wanted me to emphasize certain notes—for instance: "hahahahahaHAha-hahaHAhahaha." I never managed to fully accomplish that task. My voice teacher, Bob, told me that each "ha" is a little "push"— something you really ain't supposed to do. But, he assured me, the ensuing musical lines are legato and if I sang them purely I would immediately be okay after all those "pushes." It's not your typical musical-comedy song; it's a brilliant, scary, exhilarating aria, and I remain immensely proud that I introduced it to audiences.

Candide ran for only two months, but it acquired a cult follow-ing, and the closing-night performance was just like an opening. There wasn't a seat to be had and people were actually standing on their seats screaming: "No! No! Keep this show open!" There just weren't enough fans to keep it going indefinitely, and when the show closed I had a feeling of the rug being pulled out from under me. I always do at the end of a run. That's just how it is— especially when you have bonded with your fellow castmates. The cast, the crew, the ushers, the box office—everyone is working together with one goal in mind: to put on the best possible show. You experience a sense of belonging as soon as you walk through the stage door—you're a family. During a run your entire day is colored with the knowledge that you're going to perform the show that night no matter what. When the show closes, the entire struc-ture of your daily life is yanked away and simply vanishes over-night.

I was fortunate to receive great notices for my work in the show, and, frankly, I was surprised not to receive a Tony Award nomina-tion. Maybe it was because people just didn't know what to make of the show. When I did win the Tony Award the next year for *The Music Man* I decided that part of that award was for *Candide*.

After *Candide* a lot of people, including Bernstein, said, "You ought to do opera"; but I was never really tempted. I had a light soprano voice, and if I entered the world of opera I'd be singing Barbarina and Susanna the rest of my life. If I couldn't do *Tosca* I didn't want to play. There's just no way in hell I could sing the roles I liked—I'd kill myself trying to do that stuff. I also think the lifestyle of an opera singer is hard. There is constant, wearying travel, and you don't have the benefits of a long run, in which you can work on specifics and ask yourself, "How can I do this better tonight?" I love that kind of detailed work.

Difficult as it was to sing, *Candide* made my voice stronger. Singing the score became second nature, like breathing. Richard Wilbur made me angry years later when he was on *The Dick Cavett Show* and said I had nearly ruined my voice by singing *Candide* eight times a week. The exact opposite was true. I was singing properly, and by the end of the run my voice was stronger. And better. So there, Richard Wilbur. I was ready for my next adventure.

PEOPLE MAY HAVE been talking about the possibility of my singing opera, but I knew that I was meant for musical theater, and shortly after *Candide* I performed in a second production of *Carousel* at City Center, this time in September of 1957, as Julie Jordan, the female lead.

Before *Carousel,* however, there was a detour to television for a live broadcast of Gilbert and Sullivan's *Yeomen of the Guard.* Alfred Drake, who had become Broadway's foremost musical leading man after his performance in *Oklahoma!,* was my leading man. I was pretty nervous about the live telecast, but Alfred was even more nervous. We began the performance, I looked at Alfred, who was usually unflappable, saw terror in his eyes, and knew I needed to stay calm.

The cast included Celeste Holm and Bill Hayes, and the great Franz Allers, who had conducted *My Fair Lady* on Broadway, was our musical director, so Alfred and I knew we were in very capable hands. In the end it all unfolded quite well, and then I was onstage at City Center again, playing Julie Jordan.

I actually had a better time playing the secondary role of Carrie in the production three years earlier, because Carrie is more fun. When I was playing Julie I couldn't fool around much backstage—I had to keep myself pulled in. I think the key to the role was to remember that Billy Bigelow was a very troubled man and Julie had to be his calming influence. David gave me a terrific piece of advice when he suggested that I think of her as a cool, calm, lake. Well, as Dick and Oscar wrote, she's "quieter and deeper than a well."

Shortly before *Carousel* I found myself in Hollywood filming an episode of the television series *Alfred Hitchcock Presents*. My appearance on the show was thanks to *Plain and Fancy*; Paul Henreid had come to see *Plain and Fancy* and told me later that he had made a note in his Playbill that read "Use this girl." As a result, when he was hired to direct an episode of *Alfred Hitchcock Presents* on television, he cast me—as a nymphomaniac!

Hitchcock was not around, but Paul was very, very kind, especially to a still unseasoned television actress who was a bit unsure of herself on camera. I starred opposite Vic Morrow (who later died in that tragic helicopter accident during the filming of *Twilight Zone: The Movie*) and somehow got through the episode with Paul's kindness and David's help. The episode aired in June of 1957, right before *Carousel*, by which time I had signed for the female lead in a new Broadway musical.

I had received a call to come hear the score of this new musical, called *The Music Man*, at conductor Herbert Greene's apartment. Only one other actor was present, Andy Griffith, who was being considered for the leading role of Professor Harold Hill.

There was already a lot of buzz about the show, with people saying that the lead role was a terrific one for a singing actor. A great many people were considered, and many even tried out for it. You know who really wanted the role? Ray Bolger. Meredith Willson was not a proven Broadway composer/lyricist, however, and I have heard that the list of those who actually turned down the role was a long one: Art Carney, Gene Kelly, Bert Parks (who later actually replaced Robert Preston on Broadway), and Jason Robards.

Now, Ray Bolger was a talented man and great fun, but that casting would have been all wrong. The key to the role of Harold Hill is that he has to be sexy as hell, and one of the things that made our production of *The Music Man* work so well was that Bob Preston was an extremely sexy guy; you really could imagine that the whole town—men, women, dogs, cats, and sheep—could have fallen in love with him. That's why it was so funny when Helen Raymond, who played Mayor Shinn's wife, Eulalie, would get so flustered talking to the Professor; she fluttered around him and did this funny little bit of business with her feet because she just couldn't keep still around Professor Harold Hill. It worked because Bob Preston was pure, walking sex—and, my God, he was great in that role.

I was blown away when I heard the score for *Music Man* at Herbert Greene's apartment. That was the first time I'd heard that rhythmic singing, that speak/sing dynamite rhythm that propelled the show forward like a train leaving the station, keeps gathering speed, faster and faster, until you just surrender to the sheer glory of the movement. I really did feel all of that even when it was just Herbert singing at the piano. I was knocked out. People forget that Meredith was a conservatory-trained musician, having played in both the John Philip Sousa band *and* in the New York Philharmonic under Toscanini and Stravinsky, and that training and experience showed.

The nice thing for me was that everybody seemed to want me for the role of Marian, the River City librarian and piano teacher who falls for con man Professor Harold Hill. Even though the role seemed to be mine, Frank Loesser, who was one of the producers of the show, had asked to hear me sing. He wanted to put his stamp of approval on the whole thing, and when he said, "Sing some high notes," I just ripped off a few high C's and E's. It was just what he wanted. He seemed to like big and loud, to the point that on his studio wall he had hung a sign that read: LOUD IS GOOD, LOUDER IS BETTER. Because everyone seemed to want me for the show, I don't remember sitting by the phone wondering the usual "Oh, am I gonna get this show?" I had already worked with Morton Da Costa when he directed *Plain and Fancy*, and I think he was instrumental in helping me land the show. Tec was particularly well known for his work on straight plays, like *No Time for Sergeants* and *Auntie Mame*, but I sure had a great time with him on the two musicals we did together.

The Music Man had actually been a long time in arriving. I think Meredith worked on it for about five years, writing book, music, and lyrics, although Franklin Lacey helped him with the book (while receiving credit only for his work on the story). I think there were something like thirty drafts of the book! Tec himself also deserved credit for parts of the book, because originally the character of Winthrop, my little brother in the show, was, to use the word of the time, spastic. His big thing was going to be crashing the cymbals together every now and then, but onstage that gimmick is not as useable or funny and lighthearted as Tec's idea of having that cute little boy speak with a lisp. Tec's change was a really smart and important decision, one made even better by the fact that the young boy they cast, Eddie Hodges, was adorable. A darling kid.

I met Bob Preston briefly before we started rehearsals, and when those rehearsals began, in the fall of 1957, the show seemed to work right from the very first day. We had a great rehearsal period in which we jelled with a sense of family. In fact, one day during rehearsal Meredith came to me and said, "*Now* I know who you are. You're my *mother*. I wrote about my mother!"

Meredith was a very young-looking, handsome fifty-five-year-old at the time of the show, and he was a friendly, nice, and generous man. On opening night he gave me the most beautiful present—a heart from Tiffany. When you opened the heart you had two hearts, and when you opened that further it became a four-leaf clover. On the inside of each of those four hearts he had had engraved the beginning bars of all four of my big songs in the show. Then, when you closed the heart up, on one side it said "Barbara," and on the other it said "Marian." It was so thoughtful, the nicest opening-night gift I've ever received. He gave Bob a gold cigarette lighter, and while we think of that differently now, at the time it was a great gift.

Meredith's generosity extended to his wife, Rini, to whom he gave the most extraordinary present on opening night. It was an antique lorgnette that was encrusted with diamonds, rubies, and emeralds. There were also engraved initials, which read in order, NB to JB, JB to LR, and MW to RW. The first initials stood for Napoleon Bonaparte to Josephine Bonaparte, next came Jim Brady to Lillian Russell, and, finally, Meredith Willson to Rini Willson. The story was that when Meredith first saw this lorgnette he asked the owner if he would add his and Rini's initials. The man agreed and the initials were added. Rini was, of course, thrilled. However, the truth is that Meredith had all of the initials added and never told Rini about it. He just wanted to please her, even if he had to fib to do it.

Before we went out of town we had a "gypsy run-through" (for an invited audience of theater friends) on an empty stage with just piano and work lights. The response was enormous. Gigantic.

Even then, when the piano struck up "Seventy-six Trombones" for the final bows, rhythmic clapping from the audience started instantly. And then—the audience stood. Those jaded, seen-it-all Broadway gypsies were standing to applaud. This was in 1957, when standing ovations were rare. Now, God knows, they're *de rigueur*, no matter how good or bad the show. When we played the show, our audiences never—I mean never—failed to clap to the "Seventy-six Trombones" scored bows.

Tec gave us a big speech the next day about how just because our friends and family liked us, we shouldn't think we had it made. He told me later that the response at the gypsy run-through had scared him because he thought we might get complacent. I liked Tec very much—he was so easy to work with and gave me room to explore the character. We had only one disagreement, which occurred when he tried to show me how to put my arm around someone onstage. I disagreed strongly. You can't do that—the way we touch others is so personal, so individual. It was really no big deal, but it bothered me at the time. I said to him, "You have to back off." That was it for disagreements. The rest of the time we got on very, very well. David also helped me with the character of Marian, but he never, ever talked against the director. He would just give me really helpful notes that deepened my understanding of the role.

When we went out of town to Philadelphia, the opening number, with all of the traveling salesmen singing on the train was just not working. They'd sing, "He's a music man / and he sells clarinets to the kids in the town . . . with the big trombones and the rat-a-tat drums / Big brass bass, / Big brass bass"—it was all fully orchestrated and it just didn't land with the audience. Tec solved the problem with two terrific ideas: first, he cut the orchestra, so you could really hear the guys a capella. They supplied the rhythm and the entire song was built around that rhythm, without a single note of music underneath. In addition, Tec also had the actors jiggle up and down in their seats. They hadn't been jiggling before. Now they'd sing "To the kids in the town" and you'd see all the guys jiggling as if they were really on a train. It was electric. The audience loved it! So simple and so good. Stephen Sondheim has gone on record as stating that "Rock Island" is one of the best opening numbers in musical-theater history.

People loved the music right from the start, but Meredith made changes and even wrote a new song on the road to try and replace "Iowa Stubborn"—

> Oh there's nothing halfway about the Iowa way to treat you,
> If we treat you, which we may not do at all

I can't remember what he wrote, but it lasted exactly four performances before everyone decided it wasn't as good as "Iowa Stubborn," which went right back in.

One of my big songs, "My White Knight," kept changing. The song was originally much longer, because Meredith told me it was intended to be a kind of counterpart—a balance—to Bob's big song "You've Got Trouble." But that very long version of "My White Knight" didn't work in the scene. Meredith wrote so many variations of the song that I ended up performing twelve different versions of it. That's right—twelve. It was hard! During those out-of-town tryouts I'd go onstage thinking, "Now which version do I sing tonight?"

I was the leading lady but not the above-the-title star—I hadn't earned that yet. I knew the show represented a big opportunity for me, but Bob carried the show, no question about it, and he was sensational. He had developed a very effective manner of speaking/singing his songs, à la Rex Harrison in *My Fair Lady*. His family used to sing, and he had a great sense of rhythm and pitch, but he wasn't a trained singer. That didn't really matter because he was just so damn good onstage. He wasn't a trained dancer either, but he moved just like one onstage.

He actually had only one mishap out of town, when, in our last week in Philadelphia, he started losing his voice at the final matinee. As his voice grew weaker and weaker, he started getting kind of crazed. His standby, Larry Douglas, who was married to Onna White, our choreographer, had to finish the performance. Of course we were still out of town, so Larry hadn't been fully rehearsed. The stage manager would read a line to him offstage and then he'd say it onstage, and that's how we played the scenes on that Saturday. It was pretty crazy!

We felt we had a good shot on Broadway because the response out of town had been sensational, but you just never know. Our producer was Kermit Bloomgarden, who was also the producer of the play *Look Homeward, Angel*, which had opened in November 1957, one month before we were to open at the Majestic Theater on December 19. When we were in Philadelphia with *Music Man*, Bob showed me a telegram that Jo Van Fleet, who was starring in *Look Homeward, Angel*, had sent him right after they opened to sensational reviews; her telegram read: "Come on in, the water's fine."

Our opening night on Broadway felt like we were riding on top of a tidal wave. Kermit threw a big party at Sardi's, and in those pre-Internet days, everyone waited for the newspaper reviews. When they came in they were sensational. John Chapman in the *New York Daily News* raved that *The Music Man* was "one of the few great musical comedies of the last 26 years," comparing it to *Of Thee I Sing* and *Guys and Dolls*. Whew!

Now, sixty years later, I retain a very clear memory of going home on that opening night, and as I was opening the door of our apartment, my husband stopped me and said: "Wait a minute, do you realize what's happened? You're a hit in a hit." And of course I was thrilled. Then my next thought was, "Oh my God—now I have to do this for how long?!"

Actually, I think if you want to, you can learn a great deal from a long run. I know I did, because I had a sold-out audience of 1,600 people waiting for me every single night, and to keep myself interested I would give myself tasks. The purity of my singing—the vocal quality and simplicity of emotion—these things have always mattered to me, and one of the tasks I set for myself in a song like "My White Knight" was to sing it as simply and purely as I could, without unnecessary gesture. I'd ask myself: "Do you have the courage to just stand there and not have to do something? Can you just be there for that song, at one with the audience? Can you do that?" It's still a task I set for myself.

Once you get into the swing of a long run, the routine becomes second nature. Every day around four-thirty or five I'd get very sleepy, so I'd take a little nap. Then I'd have a light dinner before going to the theater to get ready. It was the anticipation that was hardest, but once I got started, I gave it everything I had. Before I knew it I had done the show 373 times . . . It all lies in the approach, because if you try to get by at half-speed, not only does that make the performance seem endless to you, the actor, but it also cheats the audience. I understand how and why that can happen, but when I've seen it—Streisand walking through *Funny Girl* and Merman in *Gypsy*—it's so disappointing.

When Merman was "on," however, she was electrifying. Filled with supreme confidence. For all of her bombast, she still made it seem real. She was nothing less than a thrilling force of nature. I saw *Gypsy* four or five times, both because my friend Julienne Marie replaced Sandra Church in the title role, and because that show thrilled from the start: the first thing you heard was one of the greatest overtures ever written, followed by a terrific book, the classic Styne and Sondheim score, and the great Ethel herself. When she charged down that aisle, trumpeting "Sing out, Louise!" you knew you were about to go on a great journey. What a night of theater.

And, boy, did Ethel have a mouth on her. One of her closest friends was Benay Venuta, who corroborated the following story. When Benay was Merman's understudy or standby, they would often have dinner together between shows. One day when Benay came to fetch her, Merman was putting on a turban and she was very carefully pulling out little curls all around the edge of the turban. Benay took one look and said, "Jesus Christ, Ethel, what's with the curls? Don't you know the whole point of wearing a turban is to get that sleek look?" Ethel replied, "Fuck you, Benay. It gives me softness."

And then there's this one: a friend of mine played piano in the pit for one of her shows, and during the run, the cast and all the musicians were invited to a party at the very swanky apartment of one of the wealthy Park Avenue–type ladies. Ethel and my friend happened to be leaving together when he said to her, "How kind of Mrs. So-and-So to have a party for us." Whereupon Miss Merman said, "That c--t, she's so cold you could tap-dance on her tits!"

To get back to long runs for a moment, I can't say I didn't have moments when my mind completely wandered. I can remember standing onstage in the middle of a song and realizing I had no memory of having sung the beginning of the song—I was thinking about what I was going to have for dinner or the shopping I had to do. Panic would seize me because at that moment you instantly think, "Oh my God—let me get myself back here right now! This is scary!"

I had started to think of myself as an actress first and a singer second—a big step. I hadn't received any formal training as an actress, so I learned the lines, did what was written on the page, and then tried to develop the character, bit by bit, until she became a real person. David was an enormous help to me on all of my shows and helped me see the whole character of Marian Paroo, just as he had with that of Julie Jordan in *Carousel*. However, even in *Music Man* I was still learning and made some terrible mistakes. One time Bob Preston and I were on the footbridge and I came on with my big hat and accidentally dropped it on the stage in front of the footbridge. What I should have done was find a way to pick up the hat as I left, but I didn't—I did not clean up my own mess before I left the stage. Bob had to pick up my hat and carry it off— terrible of me.

We recorded the original cast album right after we opened. Back in the 1950s the recordings were made in one day, the second Sunday off after opening. It was a marathon recording session but well worth it. The album ranked at the top of the charts for twelve weeks, won the Grammy Award for Best Cast Album, and sold one million copies, while remaining on the charts for nearly five full years—245 weeks! We received two weeks' salary for recording the album but never a cent more.

I loved working with Bob Preston. He was such a good actor that it was very easy to work off of him. I felt safe with him onstage.

We had a really wonderful working relationship, and I'm glad it didn't turn into anything more than that, because he was prone to having affairs with his leading ladies. When he did the show *Ben Franklin in Paris* there were lots of headlines about his having an affair with his leading lady. His wife, Catherine, was a beautiful, sweet woman, but she sure didn't have it easy with Bob.

Bob and I had a truly great professional relationship, and Catherine was wonderful—she had a beautiful, motherly presence. There was something very calming about her. Occasionally David and I would go out with Bob and Catherine, but not very often. I have a funny memory of going with them to a wonderful Japanese restaurant Bob kept talking about. Sashimi was a relatively new thing—remember this is 1958—and my reaction was: "Raw fish? Are you kidding? You're going to eat raw fish?!" Bob insisted, "You've got to try this." Off we went to the Saito Restaurant, which was really a kind of gourmet Japanese restaurant, complete with beautiful little private rooms. The food was superb, and during the ensuing years I grew to really love sushi and sashimi. In 1958, however, the thought of eating raw fish felt like visiting another planet.

Bob presented a very interesting dichotomy—very gregarious, seemingly open, but at the same time extremely private. Each night before the show began he would come into my dressing room and we'd talk about the day—politics, what was happening in the world, a great one-on-one conversation. And yet, after each of these encounters, he would leave and I felt as if I didn't really know him at all.

Our conversation would end, Bob would go onstage, and wow! He was sensational—funny and touching: The audience just didn't expect this staggering star turn from him. He had played sidekick to Gary Cooper in *Beau Geste* and been a second-tier Hollywood guy in films like *The Macomber Affair*. There really wasn't a lot of sexuality in his films, but onstage—whoa! Very sexy.

Bob was a great team leader because those preshow talks weren't just for me. He really did spark the company. Bob would get on the loudspeaker backstage and talk to us before the show started; it wasn't an "Okay, let's win one for the Gipper"–type speech, but rather a joke or something fun. The company adored him and he was very, very easy to get along with. When it comes from the top like that it helps the cast pull together, and as a result we had a very good company. I think Hugh Jackman was like that on *The Boy from Oz*.

Bob had it written into his contract that he and I each were allowed two-week vacations and that we could take our vacations at the same time. He said he didn't want to play the show with anybody else, and I never did play it with anyone else, except for that one performance with Larry Douglas in Philadelphia and a very few performances in New York when Bob fell ill.

And then there was David Burns, who played Mayor Shinn. He was a wonderful actor who went on to play the male lead in *Hello, Dolly!* with Carol Channing, but he was also a very raunchy kind of guy. When I think about his shenanigans now it all seems funny as hell, but at the time I got all prissy about it. Maybe it came from my husband—he didn't even like me to say "damn." God forbid I'd say "shit." At the time, I just thought, "I'm a lady, and, Davey, you don't *do* that in front of me." Miss Priss of 1957. Here's what Davey was like: Christian Dior died while we were in rehearsal; and, though I didn't actually see this firsthand, I was told that when David heard the news he tied a black ribbon around his penis and would say to the guys: "Isn't it a shame about Christian Dior?" Very funny.

When the show became such a big hit, Eddie Hodges and I sang on television's *Your Hit Parade*, which meant we were reaching millions of people across the country. And, at the same time, I also appeared on many television game shows. They were a lot of fun, and very lucrative. You did two days of work where you'd tape five shows, for which you received $1,000. That was very good money in 1958, and it's not bad these days, either.

Our show became the destination Broadway must-see for celebrities in town, and boy did I meet some fascinating people. Former President Truman came backstage with his wife, Bess, daughter Margaret, and Margaret's husband, Clifton Daniel. Bess was very motherly, and made sure everyone got to shake the president's hand. I felt the same way about Barbara Bush when I sang at the White House; they were both very warm, maternal women.

For a movie-mad youngster like myself it was a dream come true to meet my childhood idols when they stopped backstage. Dorothy Lamour turned up one night, and, ever suave, I blurted out: "You're Dorothy Lamour!" Without missing a beat she wisecracked, "Yeah, what's left of me, honey!" Best of all was Gary Cooper—the divine Gary Cooper. One night during our preshow chat Bob casually mentioned to me: "Coop's out front."

"Who?" I stammered.

"Coop. Gary Cooper is in the house tonight, Barbara."

Very calmly I said to Bob, "If I don't get to meet Gary Cooper your life isn't going to be worth a plugged nickel."

Well, the show ended, and as I was removing my makeup there was a knock at my door, and there in all his glory stood the incredibly handsome Gary Cooper.

"Oh—Mr. Cooper—I'm so happy to meet you."

His reply? "Gosh."

I was performing eight shows a week and somehow still had time to perform in a television production of *Hansel and Gretel*. I had a lot of energy in those days! The show had a score by William Engvick and Alec Wilder, and Red Buttons was my costar. If I was a little old at age thirty to be playing Gretel, Red was really stretching things as a thirty-nine-year-old Hansel! Directed by Paul Bogart, the show also featured Hans Conried, Stubby Kaye, and the wonderful opera singer Risë Stevens as the mother. With Rudy Vallee playing our father, we were definitely an eclectic cast.

Hansel and Gretel was telecast in April 1958, the same month as the Tony Awards, which were held in the ballroom of the Waldorf-Astoria Hotel. The show would have been telecast in New York, although not nationally, but there was a labor strike at that time, so there was no television broadcast of any sort. As it turned out, we were sitting at the same table as everyone from *Look Home-ward, Angel*, a group that included Jo Van Fleet. She had sent that nice telegram to Bob Preston in Philadelphia, but she was an edgy woman. Just before my category was announced, she said to me, "I've heard that you won." That is definitely not what anyone wants to hear before their award is announced. What if it weren't true? And if I were going to win, why did she take it upon herself to be the one delivering the news? Well, she was a tough cookie. I once ran into Pat Hingle when he was in a play with Jo and I said, "How is working with Jo Van Fleet?" Pat, a very sweet man, looked at me and said, "Ever been onstage with an anteater?"

They called out my name as the winner of Best Featured Actress in a Musical, and the funny thing is that while I have absolutely no recollection of what my salary was for *The Music Man*, I definitely remember what I wore to those Tony Awards. It was a beautiful, very simple dress with a flaired chiffon skirt, and a top that was all gold—very fancy and really pretty. I liked it so much that I also wore it to the opening-night party for *She Loves Me* five years later. I was very nervous when I scurried up to receive the award, and didn't actually say much except "Thank you." I suspect it was one of the shortest Tony acceptance speeches in history, but I was very pleased to have won, especially after the disappointment of not being nominated for *Candide*.

The night got even better because I wasn't the only winner from *Music Man*: Bob Preston, David Burns, and our conductor Herbert Greene all won, and the show won the biggest prize of all, Best Musical.

The big competition that year was between *The Music Man* and *West Side Story*. Of course I went to see *West Side Story* and thought the dancing was out of this world; for some reason I remember thinking that the book didn't work—I don't remember why, because I certainly don't feel that way when I see the show now. *West Side Story* was groundbreaking, no question about it. It's a brilliant show, with that incredible Bernstein music, Steve Sondheim's lyrics, the Jerome Robbins staging—wow.

People spoke about a "rivalry" between the two shows, and in the face of all that groundbreaking work on *West Side Story*, it's easy to forget how brilliantly constructed *Music Man* really is. The rhythmic sing/speak that Meredith came up with makes the show flow from the very first scene on. Interestingly enough, Meredith had actually started working with that form even before *Music Man*, back on a radio program called *The Big Show*. That show, which went on the air in November of 1950, was hosted by Tallulah Bankhead and may well have been the last big radio show before the demise of radio and rise of television. Meredith was the music director and conductor of the show, and instead of having commercials read, he came up with the idea of having a male chorus speak/sing the commercial—"Buy Camel cigarettes"—in rhythm. It was like rap—but a little cleaner.

There is no question about it—the 1950s were a great time for Broadway musicals. It wasn't just *The Music Man* and *West Side Story*. It was *Damn Yankees*, *My Fair Lady*, *Gypsy*, *Guys and Dolls*, and on and on. It's no wonder those shows are consistently revived—they are terrific musicals with strong books and first-class songs. I loved *Damn Yankees*—such a wonderful Adler/Ross score, and the great Gwen Verdon at her peak. She was a terrific dancer who oozed star quality—audiences adored her. Oddly enough, I was disappointed when I first saw *My Fair Lady*, not because I didn't think it was good—I could see how beautifully constructed it was. It's because I had heard so many details about the show from so many people that there were no surprises left. It was as if I had already seen the show before the overture even started.

As *Music Man* settled into a standing-room-only hit, I became pregnant. Deliberately so. As soon as David and I started trying, I became pregnant. We were both incredibly excited and I left the show in July of 1959 when I was about five months pregnant and really starting to show. The funny thing is that I don't remember my last performance in the show at all; I guess I was so happy about being pregnant that everything else receded. That said, I was and remain incredibly proud of my association with *The Music Man*. It wasn't just that it was a fine show; it's that rare show that really entered into the American consciousness, and thirty years later, when President Reagan left office in January of 1989, the *New York Times* ran an editorial, comparing the president to that well-known salesman, Professor Harold Hill. Remarkable.

10 · MARRIAGE, MOTHERHOOD, AND CAREER

WHEN I LEFT the show I knew I was losing a nice income, but money had never been the main focus for me, and David, who seemed to have no problem with my earning power, seemed similarly untroubled at our losing that steady income. I always felt supported by David as he helped and coached me, and while he may have felt the strain of my success, I never sensed it. I tried to be careful about money, but my joy came from performing, not making money, and when I became pregnant with my son, even performing came in a distant second.

I had grown to depend heavily on David, and before we became parents, that suited both of us. I trusted him completely, both personally and professionally, and valued his advice. Ironically, by now so, too, did my mother; David and I had been married for seven years, and with the passage of time, as she came to know the real David, she had gradually overcome her prejudices and come to respect his integrity. She actually asked for David's advice on matters ranging from finance to housing.

Aside from developing an aversion to the smell of cigars (David was a cigar smoker), it was all smooth sailing while I was pregnant, and I gave birth to my beautiful son Adam at the tail end of 1959. Motherhood seemed like the ultimate miracle to me. It still does. I remember going into labor, and driving to the hospital with David saying, "We're going to bring a new human being into the world." I was so happy to be a mother, and really thrilled to be Adam's mother. I love him so much—and besides loving him, I admire and like him. We have many of the same interests in the arts and he has been very helpful to me in dealing with finances. I am very lucky to have my son.

After giving birth to Adam, I was breast-feeding and I became interested in the nutritional advice of Adelle Davis; Adelle suggested that if you're breast-feeding, it's good to drink a Carlsberg beer because it has yeast and B vitamins. We used to buy that beer by the case, and while I'm not so sure about Adelle's nutritional theories, it did make for some interesting times while breast-feeding.

We were living in Port Washington, on Long Island, and doing pretty well as a family. There were, of course difficult moments, especially when my mother came to visit, but David, Adam, and I were a family. David was so protective of me, and at first that all felt great. He provided certainty, and when I would put my head on his shoulder he would comfort me, as a father would a child.

At the same time, the itch to perform had certainly not disappeared, and when I was offered the role of Anna in *The King and I*, I accepted immediately. In fact, if I had to choose my favorite role from my entire career, it would be playing Mrs. Anna in the City Center *King and I* revival in May of 1960.

Our King was Farley Granger, and he was terrific. There was a very healthy sexuality between our characters. Our complicated onstage relationship built and built throughout the evening until we finally touched for the first time as the music swelled up for "Shall We Dance?"; let me tell you, that moment was all about sex! We made that scene work like gangbusters, not just because it's a terrific Rodgers and Hammerstein song, but because we made the moment real: the dialogue leading into the song explained our growing attraction because we believed it and lived it onstage. David was really, really helpful to me with that show. He coached me on every scene, and I think I responded with my very best work.

I loved that role—you can't ask for more as a musical-theater actress. There was such beautiful music—"Hello, Young Lovers," "Getting to Know You"—and meaty dramatic material to boot. The critics really praised the production—the *New York Times* called it "the best performance of Miss Cook's career"—and what made it all the sweeter was the response from Rodgers and Hammerstein and their peers. Oscar and Dick sent me a note that said: "We wish last night had been the Broadway opening." To receive that sort of praise from Dick and Oscar was a very big deal for me.

Arthur Laurents, who was definitely a tough man of the theater, wrote a letter to Dick saying that it was the best production of *The King and I* that he had ever seen, and that *The King and I* had now supplanted *Carousel* as his favorite Rodgers and Hammerstein show. Arthur, who wrote the extraordinary book for *Gypsy*, said that our production made the book a "revelation . . . It's more pertinent today and, being better acted, is more real and touching. The difference is that where Gertrude Lawrence and Yul Brynner were strikingly electric personalities, Barbara Cook (what a difference her singing makes!) and Farley Granger—surprise, surprise!— are better and more honest actors. Enough gushing. It's an absolutely marvelous show and I could see it once a year."

What made all that praise even more meaningful was that Dick wrote back to Arthur, stating: "There is no question in my mind as to the justification of your feeling that Barbara and Farley are more honest and really better artists than the people who played the parts originally." That was music to my ears.

I have to say that a large portion of the credit belonged to Farley; he was excellent in the role and his vulnerability and sensitivity as a person really made you believe that at the end of the show the king's spirit has been broken. As great as Yul Brynner was, it's hard to believe anything could ever break his spirit.

I'm my own worst critic and always think I can do better, but this time both Farley and I each felt we had surpassed ourselves. I loved the role so much that I couldn't wait to get to the theater every night. There was even talk that they were going to move the production to Broadway, but there was an Actors' Equity strike and by the time it was over we had lost all of our momentum. Farley and I were able to play it one more time in an outdoor arena production in Washington, but we never made it to Broadway. I would have loved the opportunity to explore that role in depth over the course of a months-long run, but the show lives on as one of my favorite memories.

Farley and I were unable to make a recording of that production, but four years later I recorded a studio version with completely new orchestrations by Philip J. Lang. It was part of a series of stereo recordings of shows that previously had been available only in monoaural, and it was a thrill to record that gorgeous music with a full studio orchestra. The King was sung by Theodore Bikel, a man I liked a great deal, and the recording was produced by Thomas Z. Shepard, with whom I'd be reunited twenty-one years later for the Avery Fisher Hall recording of *Follies*, as well as my CD *The Disney Album*. It was great to now have a permanent record of my work.

I had so much respect for Rodgers and Hammerstein—they were geniuses, and I do not use that word lightly. I wish I had been able to originate a role in one of their musicals, but I never did. I do remember auditioning for *Pipe Dream*, but I think I had too much of a little-girl look. They wanted a more womanly look for the role of Suzy, which is what they got with Judy Tyler. It was not one of their better shows, but look at their legacy: *Oklahoma!*, *The King and I*, *South Pacific*, *Carousel*, *The Sound of Music*. They received every possible honor, and justifiably so—but I do think Oscar still hasn't received enough credit for the books he wrote. His terrific books are a big reason why their shows are constantly revived. They possess real dramatic structure and genuine conflict. The old Irving Berlin and Cole Porter shows, for all of their brilliant music, just don't possess the solid dramatic bones that Oscar gave the R&H shows.

My next role turned out to be in *The Gay Life*, a musical that opened on November 18, 1961. The show had a dazzling score, and I had a terrific role. It was the first time I didn't have to audition for a role, as well as the first time I had my name above the title. Clearly my career was entering its prime, but of course I didn't realize it at the time—you never do. You just keep working and wondering what will come along next. At the time of *The Gay Life*, however, it was all pretty heady and I was very happy.

The Gay Life was based on *The Affairs of Anatol*, by Arthur Schnitzler. There were several ladies playing Anatol's paramours, and when it became evident out of town that the show was in trouble, Herbie Ross, who had taken over the direction, suggested that I be allowed to play all the ladies. Of course I thought that was a great idea, but the creators were afraid to make such a big change. The structure of the show stayed exactly as it was, which proved fatal.

It's often hard to know exactly why shows don't work. Usually it's the book that's blamed, which makes you realize how incredibly difficult it is to write the book for a musical: just as you're building a scene to its dramatic climax, you the librettist are pushed aside so that the composer and lyricist can take over. A weak book may well have been the cause of *The Gay Life*'s quick demise, although I'm not sure. It's the same old problem: when you are in a show it's hard to judge because you live behind the curtain, inside your role. You can't really know what magic is or is not happening out front. The book for *Gay Life* was written by Fay and Michael Kanin, who had just written a first-rate screenplay for the Doris Day/Clark Gable comedy *Teacher's Pet*, but this script never caught fire. Adding to the problem was the fact that our leading man, Walter Chiari, was badly miscast.

Walter did his best, and I adored working with him. He was a dear, sweet man. He had gone through a hot, internationally publicized affair with Ava Gardner and was generally thought of as the quintessential Latin lover. God knows he was handsome enough for the role of Anatol, but what we didn't know in advance was that his greatest talent was as a comedian—he was extremely adept at improvisation—and that he possessed very little real acting technique. The net result was that if he found something that worked well in a scene, he couldn't always repeat it. In addition, his accent was quite strong, so it was hard to understand him, yet for all that, the cast loved him and so, too, I think, did the audiences.

I used to love the fight scene at the end of the show, a scene that provided me with my favorite memory from the entire show. That concluding fight scene was really a brawl—all choreographed, of course—and during the scene Walter would hold me tight, trying to keep me from "killing" Elizabeth Allen, who I thought was after my Anatol. On one particular night, as Walter was holding me, he whispered, "Bar-ba-ra, Bar-ba-ra, de pants, de pants, they are *spleeet*." He kept whispering, "De pink is showing, de pink is showing." Of course the audience was hysterical with laughter. He really worked that moment and added at least five minutes to the show. As I said, he was a great improviser.

Even with all of the show's problems, nothing can take away from the blazingly wonderful score written by Arthur Schwartz and Howard Dietz, two hall of fame songwriters who had written "Dancing in the Dark," "I Guess I'll Have to Change My Plan," and "That's Entertainment." They gave me such great songs to sing— "Magic Moment," "Who Can? You Can," "Something You Never Had Before," and "The Label on the Bottle." That last song was put in the show out of town and exemplified how terrifying working on musicals can be: I first heard the song on a Monday night right after the performance. I rehearsed it for hours on Tuesday—it was a big singing *and dancing* number, and, heaven help me, I performed it at the Wednesday matinee. I learned it fast—dance and all—and never made a mistake. I don't think for a moment that I could do that now. I've no idea how I did it then.

Sometimes shows come and go far too fast, but fortunately this extraordinarily good score is with us forever, because the original cast album was recorded. Arthur and Howard were one of the finest songwriting teams we've had, and let me tell you, they were two of the greatest guys I ever met.

The show just never caught on, however, and Kermit Bloomgarden, our producer, was utterly distraught over its failure. We didn't have a long run, closing after three months, on February 24, 1962; Kermit came into my dressing room on closing night, sat in a chair with his head in his hands, and was practically crying at the loss of $450,000, a huge amount in 1962. He kept saying to me, "My God, Barbara, half a million dollars. Half a million dollars." Nowadays, with musicals routinely costing more than ten million to produce, $450,000 probably wouldn't cover the cost of the star's wardrobe.

The Gay Life closed the same year that the movie version of *The Music Man* came out. I had screen-tested for the movie twice. Morton Da Costa was going to direct the film, and both he and Meredith Willson wanted me to reprise the role of Marian. The tests went well, although I remember having to wear a long skirt and only discovering after the test that I had worn the skirt backward throughout! But—the studio heads went with Shirley Jones, who had just won an Oscar for *Elmer Gantry* and was considered a box-office name. Shirley was good in the role, and when I recently watched the film again I enjoyed it. The problem with the movie was that there was no dirt—it was too clean. Put bluntly, the horses never shit in those streets. The movie wasn't bad—it was just . . . too clean. I think *The Music Man* is an earthy show, and that really didn't come across onscreen.

Fortunately for audiences everywhere, the real tragedy of Bob Preston not repeating his role onscreen was avoided. Warner Brothers initially felt that Bob was not a big enough name overseas and offered the role to Cary Grant, who smartly turned it down. Cary Grant was a sensational actor, but that role belonged to Bob, lock, stock, and barrel. He was great onstage, and he was great in the movie.

My next show, *She Loves Me* proved to have a much happier ending than *The Gay Life*. We opened in April of 1963 and ran for 302 performances, closing in January 1964. I had actually first heard about the show years before it happened; David and I were having dinner at Sardi's and lyricist Sheldon Harnick came over to say that he and Jerry Bock were writing a show for which I'd be perfect. That sounded great, but years went by and I forgot all about it. All I can say is that I'm glad it took them so long to get it right.

The basic story—we had a beautiful book written by Joe Masteroff, who went on to write the superb book for *Cabaret*—had previously been utilized for the film *The Shop Around the Corner* with Jimmy Stewart and Margaret Sullavan, and also for the Judy Garland/Van Johnson musical *In the Good Old Summertime*. I was to play the role of Amalia Balash, a clerk in a Budapest parfumerie who exchanges love letters with a man she has never met. When the man turns out to be her detested coworker, delicious complications ensue. It was tried-and-true material, but previous versions and all, Joe, Jerry, and Sheldon brought a completely fresh spin to the material; the first time I heard the score—sitting on a piano bench next to Jerry while he played—is one of my happiest memories. I thought it was sensational from that very first listen! Once my participation was set, I auditioned with several actors, including Tony Perkins, before Hal Prince, who was directing a show from scratch for the first time, settled on Daniel Massey as the male lead.

Hal is a terrific director and a true man of the theater. His twenty-one Tony Awards as director and producer attest to the breadth and depth of his career. I admire him greatly, but he also did not always make things easy, for one basic reason: he wants to direct every detail of your performance down to the way you crook your pinky finger. I think what he does is sit at home with a script and put it into a Moviola that runs through his head. Then, in rehearsal, what he wants to do is fit you into his Moviola. Of course, he's one of our greatest theater men, so what saves him is he comes up with great Moviolas. However, by working this way we'll never know what's missing by not allowing the actors to explore and come up with their own ideas. Having said all that, *She Loves Me* was his first time directing from scratch, and I have no way of knowing what his method is now.

Hal has gone on record as stating that the show's four leads—Daniel Massey, Jack Cassidy, Barbara Baxley, and me—comprised "four of the most accomplished, quirky and specific performers" he had ever known. In the liner notes for the cast album reissue he noted: "We fought every day. I prevailed." That's not the way I remember it. There was contention from time to time as there always is when putting a new show together. But I also remember how thrilled I was when I saw what we had to offer. I loved working with Hal—we could always see that his ideas were moving us ahead. For instance, at one point we needed to show the passage of time, so he came up with the device of having Arpad, the messenger boy, ride his bike across the stage to mark the passing of seasons: as leaves were falling Arpad would say, "Look, autumn!"; or as snow was falling, he'd exclaim, "Look, winter!" So simple, so effective.

When we first started rehearsals I had a very pretty, madrigal-type ballad to sing, but Sheldon came to me and said, "This song just doesn't advance the story. We're going to write you a new song that will further the plot, provide you with a great tune, and also give you a showstopper." My first thought was, "Good luck" . . . But—Sheldon was right. That new song turned out to be "Vanilla Ice Cream," which, along with "Till There Was You" from *The Music Man*, became one of my two signature songs. I've sung "Vanilla Ice Cream" in my concerts for years and it never fails to receive a great response. I love that song.

I became even more fond of Jack Cassidy, who at one point during our out-of-town tryouts talked to me about his frustration with the role of Stephen Kodaly, which he felt was not working for him. He explained that he was thinking of leaving the show. I said to him, "When any one of us is offstage—even when we're waiting in the wings—we are still all onstage, because the entire show is a team effort. We're like a string quartet. You have to stay." He did—and won a Tony Award as Best Supporting Actor in a Musical.

Jack was a funny, stylish, sometimes wicked man, who endured some tough times in his life. He had a breakdown in later years, and in the aftermath of that breakdown developed the sweetest, most endearing personality. We lost him much too soon—he was only forty-nine when, in 1976, he tragically died in a fire. He had always liked my singing and called me "the best singer in the world." There may not be any such thing as the best singer in the whole world, but I was very touched that, per his request, one of my recordings was played at his funeral. I miss him very much.

Daniel and I got along okay, with the exception of one major blowup during a performance. He was going through a difficult time with his wife at the beginning of our run, and I feel sure that's the main reason we didn't get along. It all came to a head during a performance when I objected to the way he grabbed me onstage during a particular scene, and I just got madder and madder during the remainder of the show. The stage manager told me, "Barbara, don't say anything now. We'll go in and see him together at the end of the performance." I worked up a real head of steam and then just as we entered his dressing room at the end of the show, Daniel looked at me and said, "You're right. I've been behaving badly and I'm sorry. It won't ever happen again." All my righteous anger melted away instantly and for the rest of the run we had a terrific relationship. I cared for Daniel very deeply and saw the difficulties he was having with both his wife and his father, the actor Raymond Massey. Raymond came to see the show one night and in front of many of the cast members he proceeded to criticize Daniel's performance in detail. It seems I was not the only one with a difficult parent . . . When Daniel died in 1998, at age sixty-four, I was very touched that his daughter asked me to sing at his funeral in London. He was a good and dear friend.

The *She Loves Me* company was a good one. Hal cast us very wisely, and audiences really loved the show, but we were overshadowed by the big brassy blockbusters of the time. We were a smaller, chamber-like show compared to say, *Hello, Dolly!*, the show that overshadowed us at the Tony Awards, and we also had much more music than did other musicals of the time. We were all a bit surprised that after our good reviews we only ran for nine months, but it has given me great pleasure to see that this little jewel of a show has only increased in stature through the years, having two major Broadway revivals in 1993 and 2016. The cast recording we made not only won the Grammy Award for Best Score from an Original Cast Show Album, but has remained in print to this day.

BY THIS TIME my career was in high gear, and even when a show flopped I remained in demand. Unfortunately, the problems that arose in my personal life started right around this time, too.

Those problems actually went back several years. When my career had first started to take off, in the early fifties, David's career was still floundering, so it was a big break when, late in 1952, George Abbott asked him to appear on a television variety show he was directing called *Showtime, U.S.A.* We were both very excited; but at the very last minute David's appearance was canceled, a turn of events that had a profound effect on him. After that lost opportunity he never again made another effort to perform his comedy routines, which was a huge loss because he was good. Really good. He didn't tell jokes, but rather performed comic characters in scenes that he wrote himself. It was exactly the sort of work that Sid Caesar did so well.

I really believe that that one canceled television appearance did something to David's basic personality—he never had the same kind of get-up-and-go after that. It exposed a very fragile place in him. In retrospect, I realize that David was like all of the men in my life who were supposed to protect me—turns out I was stronger than all of them put together, only I didn't know it at the time. The same thing happened during my decades-long association with Wally Harper, which began in 1974. As my accompanist, arranger, and friend, Wally really helped rescue me from years of unemployment; but he, too, was really a very fragile person. He had a problem with alcohol that he simply couldn't conquer.

When David lost that television appearance he shut down his performing career and settled into doing all sorts of odd jobs. He began studying with Lee Strasberg, and became an observer in the Director's Unit of the Actors Studio. He was a very, very talented man and could have been a really fine director. I emphasize the words "could have been." The problem was that he proved unwilling, or unable, to put himself on the line. He was in the Director's Unit for nearly ten years, but only observed, never participated. I can't imagine being in an atmosphere like that and not wanting to have my say. As scared as I would have been in his shoes, there's no way I'd wouldn't have said, "Let me give it a shot."

Throughout the 1950s, as I performed in *Plain and Fancy*, *Candide*, and *The Music Man*, it was David who helped me work on my characters for those shows. Somehow he was able to do it in a way that never interfered with what the director wanted from me, and other actors began to notice. "Who do you study with?" they would ask. When I told them that David coached me, they asked if he would help them, too. I suggested a number of times that he start teaching, but he kept finding reasons not to. Finally, after I asked him yet again about teaching, he said "Okay, I'll do it if you find the space and the students." I found a room with a little stage on West Forty-sixth Street in midtown Manhattan, and he was in business. The first class consisted of exactly three people.

Those three people soon became five. Five became ten. The class built because David was a very good teacher, and mad as I would get at him, I learned a great deal from him. I know that some people could not work with him because he held forth as God in that room, but he was a very fine teacher. The years studying with Lee Strasberg had given him a solid foundation—there was a lot of Method sense memory in his approach, and the knowledge I gained has continued to be a major part of my approach to singing for fifty years now. David had a great ability to see what was actually going on in a scene underneath the words; he really understood subtext and was able to help actors find the core of a scene. Sense memory has always come easily to me, and at first I didn't understand why other people didn't employ it. "Hey," I would think to myself, "it's helpful and very easy." Then it occurred to me—maybe it ain't so easy for everyone. We all have different strengths.

David's classes began to do very well. The problem was that he would not advertise. I thought a few ads in the trade papers would help considerably, but he adamantly refused—"No, I only want students who have been personally recommended or know my work through word of mouth." He simply wasn't practical, either about teaching or directing. When I tried to interest him in seeking work as a director he would always say, "I'll direct when I have complete control." I told him that it doesn't work that way; you have to earn that control—it isn't just handed to you. David didn't want to hear that.

I don't know why he felt so strongly about advertising, but I have theories. (Oh God, the desire to psychoanalyze is huge. Forgive me, but . . .) His demons, and we all have them, were such that he often felt he didn't deserve good things.

I have a rather strongly held theory about success. I've come to believe that we are as successful as we allow ourselves to be. Our inner dialogue runs along the lines of "I can have *this*, but oh, no, no, I don't deserve *that*." Case in point with David: he asked me to go shopping with him one day, for sport coats. Together we chose two beautiful tweed sport coats, but right before we finalized the purchase he said to me, "Aren't they too good? Don't they look too good?" He would only allow himself to have so much and then no more. I said, "David, you're getting the coats. Both of them."

As to this theory of mine about success—it does not just refer to David. I sure as hell include myself in this theory as well. I never knowingly held myself back, but I suspect there was always a residue of guilt about my sister that kept me from fully plunging ahead. I experienced the success that I allowed myself to have.

Another big problem in my relationship with David lay in the fact that although he complained all the time that I needed to "grow up," in fact he didn't really want me to act or dress like a mature woman. He didn't like me to wear dresses; he preferred me to dress in skirts and sweaters, like a schoolgirl. I wanted one basic black dress, but he was against it so I had to lie: I told him I needed the dress for an audition. I'm still not sure why he was so insistent. The best I can come up with is that he felt that if I dressed in a more womanly way, I would be more attractive to other men and that thought threatened him.

I was thirty years old at the time. This was not the way I wanted my marriage to work.

Motherhood had significantly changed my self-image. I know this sounds self-serving, but I realized that I had a capacity for growth that David didn't possess. I had originally been attracted to his certainty because I needed somebody to be strong and take care of me. The problem lay in the fact that what he believed about the world at age twenty-eight had not changed in the ensuing years. I felt like I was stuck in a box, which is something David's second wife later told me she felt as well. If you stay in that box you cannot develop your authentic self. This is true of many, many relationships in which one partner doesn't want the other to grow and change, and wants, almost demands, that you stay as you were when you first met. It's another way of saying, "I need you to be the way I need you to be. Period. No discussion." When I think deeply about David's need for total control, I realize that it was not just limited to me; if we attended a dinner party, David would not really participate in the dinner table conversation, but, inevitably, at the end of the party he'd finally participate by holding court, feeling the need to sum up the entire conversation for everyone's edification.

It's not as if David and I were having big fights. We did occasionally, of course, one of which featured an old pine table that we used in the kitchen at mealtimes. We had driven home one night after one of my performances and we were having a snack. I distinctly remember that as we noshed on knockwurst with mustard we suddenly got into an enormous fight. I lifted up the entire table and threw it right on top of David! There he was, sitting with a table on top of him, covered in mustard. Suddenly we both started laughing. Thank God we laughed as I tried to sponge the mustard off of him.

We had our moments, but most of the time we got along. That "getting along" actually revealed the root of our problem: we "got along" because I kept my mouth shut. I kept so much—too much—bottled up inside. I'd become furious with David, but I'd internalize it and head to his closet. Why? To go in there and throw all his clothes on the floor—and then I'd put them all right back. He never knew anything about it because I carefully neatened the closet after my tantrum. I should have spoken up about why I was so mad but I didn't. (I had a different sort of closet problem with my mother; she would come to the house while I was out and completely rearrange all my closets without asking. It was, in a word, infuriating.)

I realized after giving birth to Adam that things had changed; having my husband pat my head and say, "There, there," no longer cut it. I was a woman and responsible for the care and welfare of another human being. I was growing up. David expected me to be the same little-girl woman he'd always had, but there's no way I could continue in that role. There began a kind of emotional push-pull that was tearing us apart because I could no longer pretend to be okay with all of his rules, with not being allowed to have a dress.

It was the same thing when it came to food; I tried to remember to have radishes in the house—yes, radishes—because he loved radishes, and if I didn't have them in the refrigerator it somehow meant that I didn't care about him, that I didn't love him. I couldn't just have forgotten them the way we all forget items at the store; no, in David's mind the missing radishes were somehow symbolic of my lack of caring.

Household chores became a source of real tension. David wanted to be in charge of all home repairs and outdoor work, but after I asked him repeatedly to wash the outdoor window screens and he never quite got around to it, I washed them myself; in the process I overstepped his strictly drawn boundaries as to suitable chores for men and women. Discovering that I had undertaken the work myself, he grew livid, yelling at me: "That is for me to do, not you!" It grew worse on the day I asked him to help me pack two suitcases, work he considered suitable for a woman, not a man. He was so angered by my request that he simply looked at me and said, "I love you, but I don't like you." I was devastated.

David's exacting demands even extended to the appearance of our bed. We had a king-size bed, and because David had grown up with comforters (while I had never even seen one until we slept under one at his mother's house), I had to try and find a king-size comforter. The problem was comforters weren't a common store item in the 1950s, which made it very difficult to find the right size; in order to cover our king-size bed we had to buy two regular comforters, and David always insisted that his comforter overlay mine when the bed was made. Always. Inside I may have been thinking, "Oh fuck, first the damn radishes, now the comforters," but I didn't say anything. It was just easier to keep my head down—go along to get along. I felt even more stifled because I couldn't enjoy the great tension release of cursing out loud. I wasn't allowed to say anything. No "damn," let alone "fuck." David considered it unladylike. Inwardly I seethed.

So what did I do? Nothing smart, I can tell you that. I had a little dalliance with a coworker, an affair that did not mean a great deal to me. My coworker told his wife, and she informed him that she was going to call David. I stupidly decided I should tell David first. How cruel of me. His reaction was awful to see. David was a deeply moral person, and on some level I knew he would not be able to handle the information. I begged him to forgive me, to allow us to go back to the way our marriage used to be. Of course that was impossible—there's no way we could really be together after that, but we lived and slept together for four horrific years after my confession. Of course, the wife never called David and I never really *had* to tell him.

Now, I think this is all something I unconsciously set up: I was deliberately trying to end my marriage. Point is, if that's not what you have in mind, you should just keep your mouth shut. A little piece of advice here: if you do have an affair, live with your guilt and don't tell your spouse. Years down the road, I have often wondered if my having hurt him so terribly with this brief affair may have expiated some of his guilt about success so that now he could allow himself to experience good fortune. What I do know for sure is that after I told him about my affair he suddenly advertised and became a very big New York acting teacher, one making a great deal of money.

As the tension in our marriage increased, alcohol slowly but surely began to appear with increasing frequency. As it usually does, it started off in a very low-key manner. On Saturday nights when I was in *The Music Man*, for instance, I would allow myself a little treat: some very sharp cheddar cheese, popcorn, and one beer. Occasionally I'd have two bottles of beer. I'd notice it the next day, but that didn't stop me. David himself was not a big drinker, but he did like a scotch or two.

The combination of liquor with one of my mother's visits always caused problems. In truth, even after she had moved north late in 1951, months would pass when we would not be in touch. I know that must have been very painful for her because I was her life. She never had many friends in New York; she had her work as a switchboard operator and she had some friends in her office. That's it. She didn't go to movies or plays, nor did she go out to dinner with friends. She worked, she took care of her little dog, and she slept. My God she slept, sometimes up to twelve or fourteen hours a day on the weekends. Now I look back and I believe she was not well, but then I just thought that no matter how often I tried to have a good relationship with her she was simply too difficult and so very unpredictable.

It didn't help that she used to just show up without telling us she was coming, which is what she did on one particular summer day in the early 1960s. We were outside working—I was gardening, which I really enjoyed, and David was taking care of the lawn, his favorite thing. But on the day in question when my mother showed up unannounced I was also drinking scotch—boilermakers, to be precise. Scotch with a beer chaser. Jack Cassidy had taught me how to drink boilermakers during *She Loves Me*, and there I was, planting the petunias, drunk, falling over backward and laughing.

My mother was appalled.

These visits from my mother made all of the problems in my marriage loom ever larger, because her mere appearance would ratchet up the tension level. I began to realize that my interaction with my mother mirrored the one she'd had with her own mother.

Sometimes we would get along well, but eventually our times together would end badly—a big blowup of one sort or another that would send my mother sulking back home while I tried to repair the damage done to my home life.

Hindsight is always twenty-twenty, but it's clear to me that as my mother aged she became seriously paranoid. I hesitate to put a label on her condition. In the twenty-first century we know a great deal more about these problems, and perhaps nowadays she could have been helped medically. In the early 1960s, however, we didn't know enough to call her depressed or paranoid. We just called her incredibly difficult to be around.

Logic was lost on my mother; she became convinced that the people who lived in the apartment above her were banging on the floors at three in the morning night after night in order to disturb her—

"But, Mom, if they're getting up at three or four o'clock in the morning every day to annoy you, don't you think that's disturbing their sleep, too? Why would they do that?"

"The landlord is paying them to do it."

"What on earth for?"

"He wants to get rid of me."

Round and round we'd go—arriving back exactly where we started.

She waged a constant war with the superintendent of her building—when she wasn't telling me that he was her best friend. If she decided that he had done something she didn't like, he was going to be in trouble, or, more to the point, bereft of tools; when he left tools lying around in the hallway she would steal them, and in the process accumulated a cache of his tools, which she hid away in one of her closets. She certainly didn't need or want the tools. What she wanted was simply to annoy the super.

I loved my mother, and there were times we'd have fun and get along very well, but it's the bad times that stick out in my mind because they were so hurtful, going all the way back to her making me believe I had killed my sister and caused my father to leave us.

I genuinely felt sorry for her, and tried to remember what a friend said to me when I was complaining to her about my mother's behavior; she looked at me and said, "At least she stuck around when you were a kid. She didn't run away, no matter how tough her life was." That's true, and I knew that she loved me. The problem was that I became her life—her whole life. There were no boundaries where she and I were concerned. I was a part of her. She owned me, and as a result she could infuriate me in a way no one else could.

The tension with my mother only added to the increasingly evident strains in my marriage, strains that could no longer be glossed over for one big reason: I had fallen deeply in love with a married man. This was not like my previous and brief affair, which had hurt David so deeply. This was a love affair of genuine feeling and deep emotion and was to develop into the most important relationship of my adult life. I had met my soul mate.

ARTHUR HILL AND I met in 1964 when my marriage was starting to crumble and we were working together on the musical *Something More!* It wasn't a good show, even though the creative team was first rate: music by my old friend Sammy Fain, lyrics by Marilyn and Alan Bergman, book by Nate Monaster. The problem was that Jule Styne was directing, and he just was not a good director. (Although Jule retained the final credit as director, he was replaced by Joe Layton, who was a dream.) Jule could be tough to work with, but he could also be a very funny man. One day during our out-of-town tryout, we were in a technical rehearsal and a fellow who had maybe three lines in the show was acting up a storm until Jule, who was out in the house, yelled, "No, George, no! Don't act. Just rehearse."

The show tried out in Philadelphia, but lasted a mere eleven days in New York City at the Eugene O'Neill Theatre. I had found much more luck at the O'Neill with *She Loves Me* the previous year, but *Something More!* brought Arthur into my life, and for that I remain very grateful.

Arthur was a very respected actor, an elegant, lovely man who had won a Tony Award for Best Actor in a Play for his work in *Who's Afraid of Virginia Woolf?* We liked each other immediately and enjoyed working together. I was very drawn to him but I didn't know the nature of his feelings for me. We were in the midst of our

tryout in Philadelphia, and one night we had a friendly drink together after the show at the Variety Club, which was a haven for
actors. He said he would walk me back to my hotel. We left the
club and were walking down the hotel hallway when he suddenly
grabbed my arm, swung me around and kissed me, saying, "I've
wanted to do that for weeks." It was a scene out of every romantic
film you've ever seen.

There is no question that when things go wrong in a marriage
and the romance has vanished, it is very difficult not to feel twinges
when you are performing with a romantic leading man; you can
feel twinges even in passing with someone who is not your leading man. When Duke Ellington, a very handsome man, stared at
me with his beautiful eyes and said, "Miss Cook, I have always
admired your work," and kissed my hand—well, I definitely felt
several twinges.

But—my relationship with Arthur was not a passing fancy in
any way. This was the real thing, and we fell deeply in love. We
actually talked through all of the repercussions before we made
love because we both sensed that our bond was so deep that once
we made love we'd be sunk. We did, and we were. We simply fell
head over heels in love with each other.

That night was the beginning of a relationship that lasted
for several years. Arthur, along with David and Wally Harper,
became one of the three biggest male influences in my life. He was
a true gentleman in every sense of the word. He liked women and
in those pre–women's movement days treated us with respect and
courtesy. He loved books and awakened my intellectual curiosity.
He itemized every book he read along with comments about them,
and made lists of books he thought I'd like. He made me realize
that I was smart and that I possessed genuine intellectual curiosity.

He taught me about myself, giving me a sense of worth and self-respect that I had never known before.

Arthur told me that I was smart, a straightforward appreciation which contrasted with the musical "love affair" I later developed with Wally Harper. Wally loved my talent, and while he told that to many other people, in all our years together, he never once said that to me. Arthur had no problem simply telling me that I was smart, and that he loved me.

He also gave me a great piece of practical advice about furthering my education, advice which really hit home since I had never attended college. It was the 1960s, the Vietnam War was raging, and everyone was uncertain about the course of world events. I felt a bit at sea intellectually. Arthur simply said to me: "Why don't you read the *New York Times* every day cover to cover. You will receive a terrific education." I did both—read the *Times* religiously, and received a great education in the ways of the world. He was the exact opposite of David, who needed me locked away in a box under his control. Arthur was handsome, charming, and when we'd meet he would look at me, smile, and ask, "How's my girl?" I would—there's no other word for it—melt.

We tried a number of times to stop seeing each other, but we failed again and again because we loved each other so intensely. We'd part for months, and then one of us would break down and we'd get back together. It was an extraordinary, beautiful time, but oh—so—painful. My feelings were so intense that it was the only time before my participation in the ill-fated musical *Carrie* that I kept any sort of diary. Just writing a bit helped me to understand some of my feelings.

Arthur had said that if the time came when it was more painful to stay than to go away, then he'd leave, and that time finally came. We were locked in an impossible situation because he was not going to leave his wife and children; unlike me, he was in a good marriage. Being so head over heels in love with somebody is both exhilarating and devastating. He did the right thing in not marrying me—it would not have been a good idea—but at the time that's exactly what I wanted more than anything in the world and I was devastated.

Both Arthur and his wife ultimately died of Alzheimer's—his fine, beautiful mind was stilled by that insidious disease. I look back on our time together with so much gratitude, but I regret that after we parted I never had a final conversation with him in which I could tell him how much he had done for me, how much he had helped me. Once on a long plane ride I started writing a letter to him. Perhaps it was the thought of revisiting those intense emotions or the fact that I didn't want to upset the balance of his marriage, but I never sent the letter.

Arthur did nothing less than change my life and inform my art. Sometimes in life you gain and lose at the same time.

I THINK THAT I started to drink as a result of the emotional distress I was feeling in my marriage. By now Adam was four years old and the marriage had really begun to fall apart. My drinking began to increase, even when I was in rehearsals for a new show. I discovered Armagnac. I'd have some brandy but I'd still also drink beer. I then graduated to martinis. I started with Smirnoff vodka martinis and then moved on to gin martinis. I didn't realize it while it was happening, but I got to the point where I needed something at the end of the day, and needed it every single day. A Gibson. Make that two or three. Sherry while I made dinner. A post-dinner Armagnac. The list grew.

It didn't frighten me. I thought, "Well, I've got problems. I'm upset, yes, but . . ." I didn't think I was out of control. Of course that's precisely what happens with everybody who becomes a drunk. You just don't know when it happens. You cross over the line, and in my case one day while I was looking the other way I became an alcoholic. It took me a long time to recognize that monumental but simple fact.

It's not incidental that around this time I became very good friends with Maureen Stapleton. She was certainly one of the all-time great actresses, and I liked and respected her very much, but we also understood each other on yet another level, because we both had major drinking problems.

The basis of our friendship resided in my profound respect for her brilliant talent. In fact, when I was rehearsing *Flahooley* and was completely clueless about acting, our director, Daniel Mann, had told me, "If you really want to see the finest acting around, go see Maureen Stapleton in *The Rose Tattoo*." I had never witnessed anything like it. It all welled up out of her—though I bet she would not have been a great teacher. She'd have that same reaction I have about sense memory for my singing: "Why don't other people just do this?" In fact, when our mutual good friend the actor Bill MacIntyre once asked Maureen about her technique, she took the Spencer Tracy approach in answering the question: "Learn the lines and don't bump into the furniture." Billy believed she really didn't know how it all flowed out of her. It was pure brilliance, based on impeccable instincts.

Maureen cared intensely about her work, to the point where shortly before she would go onstage each night she would throw up from nerves; she wanted to make sure that her performance was as good as she could possibly make it, that she gave her all. The fear that she wouldn't measure up drove her.

It didn't matter whether the play or movie itself was good— Maureen always was. I recently happened to watch the movie *Airport*, and even in the midst of that not-so-great film she delivers a characterization that starts down at her toes. It's like it comes up from the earth—textured, deep, and instinctive.

But back in the late 1960s, we shared a joint overreliance on alcohol. I remember meeting her on the street one day, and saying, "Maureen, you know something . . . I think I've got it figured out. You just drink wine. You only drink wine." And I meant it—just drink white wine and you'll be okay. Maureen looked at me and said, "Barbara, do you know how much wine you can drink?!"

My handsome father in his World War I cavalry uniform.

Striding down the streets of Atlanta with my mother—and already in a New York state of mind.

Mrs. I. W. Curry's dance troupe
entertaining at Fort Benning,
Georgia, army base, 1944.

Tamiment, Pennsylvania, 1950.
The best possible summer stock
experience—and where I met my
husband.

Flahooley, 1951. My first Broadway show—with the Bil & Cora Baird Puppets.

Ali Hakim and Ado Annie. Touring in *Oklahoma!* with my husband, David LeGrant. *Photofest*

Backstage at the Blackhawk Hotel in Chicago with David, touring in *Six on a Honeymoon*. I'm still not sure why he had those bandages!

As Carrie in *Carousel*—even more fun than playing the lead role of Julie. *Photofest*

Plain and Fancy—the show that
put me on the map. I still have the
wedding caps a lovely Amish woman
sent me. *Photofest*

Candide rehearsals with our director,
Tyrone Guthrie. *Photofest*

Singing Leonard Bernstein's showstopping "Glitter and Be Gay" in *Candide*.

Publicity photo from the 1956 television production of *Bloomer Girl*, complete with Shirley Temple curls.

With the adorable Eddie Hodges as Winthrop in *The Music Man*.

Robert Preston: the first, best, and sexiest Professor Harold Hill.
Photofest

I loved being onstage with Robert. *Photofest*

As Amalia Balash in *She Loves Me*—a jewel of a show.

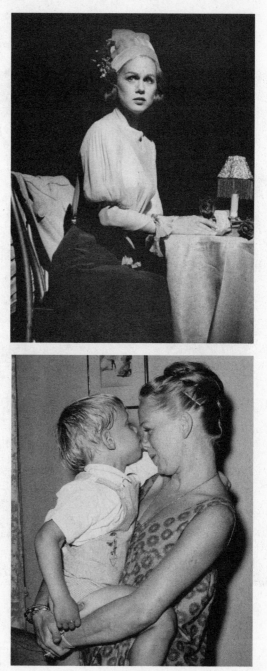

My beloved son, Adam, age three, on a hot New York summer afternoon.

Cutting up in
The Gay Life
with Walter
Chiari, 1961.

Start of rehearsals
for *Something
More*. Arthur Hill
and I soon fell
deeply in love.

One of my many appearances on *The Bell Telephone Hour*. I look like Mimi in *La Bohème*! *Photofest*

With Don Porter in the long-running comedy hit *Any Wednesday*. *Photofest*

1975: I had gained so much weight and was still drinking—but was on my way back. *Courtesy of George Connelly*

With my musical soulmate, Wally Harper. *Courtesy of Mike Martin*

With Stephen Sondheim and Elaine Stritch, signing copies of *Follies In Concert*.

Concertizing around the world throughout the 1980s and 1990s. A brand-new life. *Courtesy of Mike Martin*

Celebrating my eightieth birthday by singing with the New York Philharmonic. *Courtesy of Stephanie Berger*

Adam escorting me to the Kennedy Center Honors, December 2011. *Courtesy of Margot Schulman*

Posing with President and Mrs. Obama at the time of the Kennedy Center Honors. Thrilling. *White House Photo*

With Vanessa Williams in *Sondheim on Sondheim*, my first Broadway musical in thirty-nine years. *Courtesy of Richard Termine*

October 2012: My eighty-fifth birthday concert at Carnegie Hall with my friends (*left to right*): Josh Groban, Susan Graham, John Pizzarelli, Jessica Molaskey, and Sheldon Harnick. *Daniel Zuchnik/Getty Images*

Oh God, she was such a funny woman. Here are some of my favorite gems from the wit and wisdom of Maureen Stapleton:

—She had just broken up with some guy and was very upset, drowning her sorrows with a friend at Sardi's. It got later and later, until only the waiters and Maureen's table were left. Desperate to go home, her waiter came over and asked, "Will there be anything else, Miss Stapleton?" Maureen looked up and said, "How about a mercy fuck?"

—At some point she needed to be in London to do a play and because she was terrified of flying, she planned to take a ship. She was talking to Carol Lawrence about this trip and Carol said, "Maureen, don't be ridiculous. Fly Air France. You'll be there in no time at all and you'll have a wonderful time on the way. As soon as you're seated, they'll hand you a cocktail, then Champagne with a great meal, and after you've finished eating, a delicious digestif. Don't be silly, just fly Air France." Maureen looked at Carol and said, "Honey, I wouldn't fly Air Christ!"

I'd go out at night with friends, drink to excess, and be lucky to escape without serious injury. The night I remember most clearly? I was out with a group of friends and we were traveling from one party to another. I was packed into a car with a lot of other people, and Farley Granger was following us on a motorcycle. We stopped for a red light and I opened the door—I told myself it'd be easier to talk to him that way. Well, the next thing I knew, I had tumbled out of the car and into the middle of the street. Drunk out of my mind and laughing all the way. Not so funny.

I was still working at this point and in 1964 I played *The Unsinkable Molly Brown* for two weeks in stock. Meredith Willson had written a great score, and back in 1960 he had called me in to audition when Tammy Grimes, who was playing Molly, was having trouble with her voice. My audition was sensational, and Meredith was ecstatic. Dore Schary, the director, told me it was the best audition he'd ever seen. However, the producers, Lawrence Langner and Armina Marshall, said Tammy had an ironclad contract and it would cost them too much to break it. The talk of my taking on the role went no further. Tammy was absolutely wonderful as Molly, but oh, how I wish I had been the one to open that show on Broadway. It would have put my career on a whole different level. Of course, I am forever grateful for the wonderful shows I did do, but I was never the "big cheese." I was never "The Music Man" or "Molly Brown."

Things were turning sour between David and me, and as our problems began to seem insurmountable, I took to asking myself exactly why I had chosen him in the first place. I actually think I chose him because I knew he would never leave me like my father had. I didn't realize this at the time, of course, but now, after approximately fifteen thousand years of therapy I do.

In February of 1965, I took over the lead in the Broadway play *Any Wednesday* when Sandy Dennis left. It was rewarding to be accepted as a dramatic actress in a straight play. Because I sang well, there was always a tendency to give me short shrift as an actress, which is often true for singing actors. When people expressed surprise at my acting, I always wanted to say, "What the hell do you think I was doing all those years between songs?" The truth is, however, that I missed the music. I missed the excitement of hearing an overture. And I really missed singing.

As it was, however, when I found out I was being hired for a big hit like *Any Wednesday* and realized I'd have a nice long run with money coming in, I knew now was the time to finally leave David. We separated in 1965, when Adam was five. Just as I knew would happen, when we stood in the driveway of our house in Port Washington on that last day of our living together as husband and wife, I was the one who had to walk away. When I explained to Adam what was happening, that his father and I would be living separately but that he would still see his father, Adam cried. Just once. He curled up in my lap, cried over losing his father, and then stopped.

Adam and I moved out of our house in Port Washington into a beautiful penthouse apartment in Manhattan. Thinking now about that time, I remember the butterflies in my stomach—the fear—the oddness of not having anyone by my side to depend on. It was all up to me. I had always brought the money in, but David had been so dependable—"The Rock." My uncertainty was compounded by the fact that throughout all of this time I was drinking too much. I never drank before I worked—that would have scared the hell out of me. I saved my drinking for after the show, but it began to take a real toll. I grew so irrational that I developed a genuine fear that someone in the audience was going to shoot me while I was onstage. I had become afraid of the audience.

My mother, of course, was still on the scene, and still as difficult as ever. Right after I moved back into Manhattan, she offered to come over and look after Adam while I continued to unpack boxes. My mother was a terrific baker—in fact when we lived in Atlanta she would bake Christmas cakes for people in order to earn extra money—so when she suggested that she and Adam make a cake together I loved the idea. This, I thought, is a great Norman Rockwell moment. Adam loved helping both his father and me whenever we were cooking, and he went happily off to the kitchen with his grandmother. About fifteen minutes later he came wailing out of the kitchen:

"Mommy, Mommy, Grandmother won't let me stir the cake."

I went in to see what was going on, only to be greeted by my mother screaming, "He wants to stir the cake to the left. The cake must be stirred to the right!" My mother was screaming like a banshee over how her five-year-old grandson was stirring cake batter in the wrong direction . . . Adam adored his grandmother, and she became especially important to him after my marriage to David disintegrated, yet she thought nothing of saying in front of him, "I'm through with New York! I'm moving to London." Adam was devastated, and far too young to understand that she had no intention of doing any such thing.

As we grow up, and older, we have to face the facts that our parents are flawed human beings just like the rest of us. It has taken me years to acknowledge the fact that both my mother and my father, for different reasons, led tragic lives. After my father's severe stroke in 1952 he was never able to work again. He lived on, sometimes very happily, until he died at the age of sixty-nine, but his life was never easy. It's sobering for me to grasp that I have already outlived my father by nearly twenty years, and to realize that after he left my mother, even his second marriage was difficult. His wife, Dot, was a severe alcoholic, the kind who will drink shoe polish if that's all she can find. She finally died of alcoholism, but she was a nice woman and I always liked her. Right after she married my father she gave me a lovely little bracelet, perfect for a young girl: a little gold bracelet with tiny blue forget-me-nots on it. I adored it. It was missing one day, and when my mother saw me searching frantically for it, she told me that she had thrown it away. She owned me, right? She could do anything she wanted, either with me or with things that belonged to me—we were one, weren't we?

When David and I finally parted, he was not only free from this consistent strife with my mother, but also seemed to have been unshackled in some way. At first he was living in a grungy little room, but once he started advertising his classes he began making good money, which allowed him to find a really nice place to live, a very attractive apartment. He even hired a decorator, in essence finally giving himself permission to *have*.

I was still appearing on television during these years, and sang several times on Perry Como's popular television show between 1963 and 1965. Perry could be difficult with people, because he liked to keep everyone off balance, but I had no problems with him at all. However, singing a duet with Perry was not easy, because he sang so softly that I had to make an effort to keep my volume down in order to blend with him. Of course that soft relaxed style of his was made for television; the camera and microphone picked up the slightest gesture and inflection, and "Mr. C" was a welcome guest in living rooms across America.

It was around this time—1966, to be precise—that I experienced the first of what would, unfortunately, be many debilitating panic attacks. There was no warning sign about that first attack—it just appeared like a bolt out of the blue. My divorce had just been finalized and I was playing at Lincoln Center's New York State Theater in *Show Boat*. The panic attack was not related to the show because I really enjoyed playing Magnolia and singing that magnificent Kern and Hammerstein score. The notices were very good, and in truth the only trouble I had on the show was with my leading man, Stephen Douglass. Stephen was a very good-looking man and his singing was fine, but his acting was not. Our scenes dragged where they should have popped, and I began to resent him. It wasn't his fault—he just wasn't up to the demands of the role.

That conflict aside, *Show Boat* proved to be a first-rate experience, but when I think about the show now I still think about that first panic attack. I was in the midst of a really difficult time with Arthur, and, knowing deep down that we were not going to be permanently together, I went on a first date with another man—a very nice guy. We went to the Ginger Man restaurant, but before we ordered, I said to him, "You know, I just can't get enough air in here. Can we go outside for a moment? I'm having trouble breathing." We stood for a minute outside, but it only got worse, and I said, "I'm sorry, I'm so embarrassed, but I really think I have to go home. I feel terrible." A few moments after we got in a taxi, I said, "I'm afraid you'll have to take me to the hospital. I have a pain running down my arm and I think I'm having a heart attack."

We went to the ER and the intern on duty told me, "You're okay. You've having a panic attack." He gave me a tranquilizer. I then called my therapist and said I needed to see him immediately. My date then took me to my doctor and waited while we had a little session before taking me home. What a fun date for that poor man. He was extremely nice, but this did not exactly bode well for any great relationship ahead.

What made the attacks even more frightening was that I could never figure out a trigger. It wasn't performance anxiety. No, I could be sitting watching television or reading the paper and the attack would just whack me. I didn't see any help out there, because back when this was happening to me, people didn't talk about problems like this. Now there are books about it in every bookstore, but at the time I really didn't understand what was happening.

I was beginning to gain weight at this time, and I turned down a lot of the scripts that came to me. I did, however, appear in a 1967 production of *Funny Girl*, and one of the best things about doing that show was having George Hamilton opposite me as Nicky Arnstein. He had recently received a lot of bad press when he was dating President Lyndon Johnson's daughter, Lynda Bird, and I didn't know what to expect when we started rehearsals.

Well, let me tell you—he is so bright, so funny, so generous, and one of the best raconteurs I've ever known.

He had a very healthy view of what he had to offer as an actor and was one of the hardest workers I've ever encountered. I admired him and loved working with him. He recently came to one of my performances and it was great to see him again. I made the mistake of admiring a bracelet he was wearing. "Oh," he said, "I want you to have it," and he put it on my arm. So generous.

Funny Girl also brought me one of my favorite comments I ever received from a fan. Mark Rosen, who had entered my life during *She Loves Me*, was a very devoted fan, and would come see me in anything I did. We became friends and remain so to this day. Now, if there is any role for which I don't seem terribly well suited, it would have to be Fanny Brice in *Funny Girl*. Fanny was a fast-talking Jewish New Yorker from Brooklyn—I was a Protestant girl from Atlanta, Georgia, who loved Jeanette MacDonald and Nelson Eddy. Mark, of course, came to see me in the role, and when the film version came out in the fall of 1968 Mark rushed off to see it. He'd never seen Streisand onstage as Fanny. He called me after he saw the film. I was quite curious: "How was it?" I asked. "How was Streisand?" Mark didn't miss a beat: "Too thin, and too Jewish."

I also appeared on Broadway in Jules Feiffer's play *Little Murders* in 1967, which I remember as my first experience with the newly emerging freedom regarding sex and language. I can still remember the first time I heard the word "shit" onstage. It was in the play *J.B.* by Archibald MacLeish, and in 1959 it was shocking to hear that word uttered on the stage. Now, a mere eight years later, when I appeared in *Little Murders*, the "shits" were flying left and right. I felt very uncomfortable speaking that way onstage. My character, Patsy Newquist, was also a smoker, and I'd never smoked in my life, so I was very concerned about looking like a real smoker. I found that in order to be comfortable with a cigarette onstage, I had to learn how to handle a cigarette offstage, and also how to curse like a sailor. Hmmm . . . that may have been the beginning of what I have become: a dirty-mouthed old lady.

Unfortunately our production didn't work and we closed after seven performances, but Jules's play is a fascinating one and I'm so glad that a later production did very well.

By the late sixties and early seventies, rock and roll had permanently altered the musical landscape, dominating the music charts, taking over television, and even trickling down to Broadway, the last remaining stronghold of the Great American Songbook. *Hair* and *Jesus Christ Superstar* had opened on Broadway, and everyone talked about *Hair* as a game-changer in the Broadway musical-theater landscape. The truth is, at the time I was only vaguely aware of this talk because I did not see many of the shows—I had started to drink heavily and my interest in theater had waned, both as an actress and as an audience member.

After *Little Murders* I did appear in one more Broadway musical, *The Grass Harp*, but it ran for only four days in November of 1971. The show was based on Truman Capote's novel of the same name, and centered on an orphaned boy and two elderly ladies who observe life from a tree. Even though the show was a flop, I remain grateful that I had the chance to meet and work with Truman. He was very nice to me, very much the Southern gentleman: I met him at his apartment and we talked about furniture and literature. On that same afternoon he even introduced me to the joys of Blackwing pencils, the soft lead pencils that Stephen Sondheim uses while composing. When our meeting was through, he insisted on walking me to the elevator.

While I know that Truman could be difficult with others, he was always very kind to me. I was happy that he liked my performance, short-lived though it was. I actually enjoyed performing in the show, a lot of which took place in the tree where the three leading characters took refuge. The truth is, I fell in love with that great tree. When we closed, as much as anything, I hated to lose that tree.

Our director was theater veteran Ellis Rabb, and it was Ellis's idea that none of us would be miked. Carol Brice, Karen Morrow, Rusty Thacker, and I all had big voices, and we filled the theater. It was fun for all of us, but the audiences did not respond. I think it was just too rarified, too precious for a general audience. Although I couldn't have foreseen it at the time, this show was to be my last appearance in a Broadway musical until *Sondheim on Sondheim* in 2010.

I did, however, appear onstage in one other drama, a 1972 production of Maxim Gorky's *Enemies*, at Lincoln Center's Vivian Beaumont Theater; it ran for its allotted time of two months, but there was never any talk of an extension. My reputation, of course, is based on my work in musicals, and I'm glad the cast recordings preserve my work not just in hit shows like *The Music Man* but also in studio versions of classic shows like *Show Boat*, *Carousel*, and *The King and I*. At the same time, however, I wanted to prove that I was an actress, and appearing in *Any Wednesday*, *Little Murders*, and *Enemies* not only challenged me as an artist but also reinforced my acting credentials.

The problem lay in the fact that during most of my time in those plays I was unhappy because of the turmoil in my personal life. In the beginning of this period, when my drinking problem wasn't quite as severe and work was still a possibility, I would find something wrong with every script I was sent. When I later saw the plays I had been offered, I realized that they were respectable and I could have made something of them, but at the time I was not thinking rationally. George Abbott—Mr. Broadway—the most important musical director of the time, had one particular show he was interested in me doing, but I put him off, over and over again. I wouldn't give an answer, so of course he eventually looked elsewhere. Compounding the problem was the fact that I was also now entering the time in an actress's career that I call "middlelescence"—too old to play the ingénue, too young to play the wise, feisty older woman. I was nowhere.

I was no longer appearing in long-running musicals, and *Little Murders* and *Enemies* had closed quickly, a state of affairs that led to a financial crunch. With no money coming in I didn't say to myself, "I have to stop drinking or my career will vanish." No—in my mind, less money simply meant that I should give up fancy liquor and begin drinking Gallo Mountain Chablis, by the halfgallon. I'd drink almost all of that big jug, pour out whatever was left, and vow I would not do that "tomorrow." Come four or five in the afternoon, I would order another half gallon and off I'd go, day after day after day.

Adam and I were living in a beautiful three-bedroom apartment on the Upper West Side of Manhattan, a penthouse with a wraparound terrace, working fireplace, major ceilings, large dining room, maid's room, and good-sized kitchen. It was fantastic. I was penniless when it went co-op, but a friend loaned me the money to buy it; this was 1968, and the apartment cost $15,000. Fifteen thousand dollars wouldn't even buy a closet now. This apartment was in one of the first co-op buildings in Manhattan, and hard as it is to believe, you could not get a loan on a co-op because banks didn't give loans for co-ops in 1968. I also had no credit as Barbara Cook, only as Mrs. LeGrant. I couldn't get a credit card from Bloomingdale's because I was an unmarried woman.

I was also unemployed and a drunk—not a nice, ladylike drinker, but a drunk. I just stayed home and got drunk every night by myself. In the kitchen, dirty dishes were piled everywhere. There was a wastebasket underneath the basin in the bathroom that Adam and I shared, and at some point the wastebasket got filled and didn't get emptied. Next, the floor around the wastebasket got covered and didn't get cleaned up until the Kleenex was all the way up to the bottom of the basin—the whole corner of the room was filled with Kleenex. I would say to myself, "Why can't you clean this up?" And then I would think, "Why don't you just try to move three pieces? Just three." I just couldn't do it. I was paralyzed, and that paralysis was both physically and emotionally painful.

Weekends were the worst because that's when Adam would stay with his father. The left side of my king-size bed would be piled with books and weeks-old newspapers. As soon as Adam left I would walk to the library to return the previous weekend's books, and take out as many new books as I could cradle in my arms. I was terrified of running out of reading material because if I could keep my attention focused on a written page—of almost anything—I figured I could get through another weekend.

My life was a complete mess. I didn't shower or brush my teeth for days at a time. I couldn't imagine cooking a meal, or writing out checks, or going to sleep without liquor. It never occurred to me that alcohol was the problem. I thought if I could just work out some of my difficulties I wouldn't have to drink. I could not and would not accept the fact that I couldn't fix anything until I stopped drinking. In this regard I was no different from any other heavy drinker; there is a complete and total nonrecognition that alcohol is the problem.

Most of the people close to me drank. That's not surprising because I think when you have that problem you tend to surround yourself with people who drink. Alcoholism ran in my family—four of my mother's siblings were alcoholics—and when, in addition, you have an addictive personality, the desire to take a drink when you get in trouble is that much stronger. There is no one moment to which I can point and say, "Ah-ha—this is when I became an alcoholic." It was a gradual process. I don't remember anybody around me, besides my mother, talking to me seriously and saying, "You really ought to see if you can cut this out."

My mother was very upset about my drinking, but by this time she had zero credibility with me. Always trying to fix things and run my life, she even called a man I used to date in Atlanta and talked to him about my problem; I think he was the man my mother had always wanted me to marry, a fellow I liked as a person, but to whom I had no physical attraction. He was an acquaintance, nothing more. She called him up and said: "Barbara is in terrible trouble, she's an alcoholic. Can you help her do something about it?" He called me, and of course I replied, "Don't be silly. Sure, I drink, but I'm not an alcoholic." What I didn't know at the time was that although he was a successful attorney, he was a major alcoholic himself and subsequently died from the disease.

I was very angry with my mother at what I considered a terrible invasion of my privacy. I didn't even think I was in deep trouble, but of course I was. In hindsight I realize that, clumsy as my mother's attempt at help was, she was acting out of genuine concern. The problem was that I wasn't listening—she could have told me anything and I simply wouldn't have heard it.

This brings up the question of therapists and why they didn't help me with my drinking. I saw my first therapist when my marriage began disintegrating, before I became an alcoholic, but he soon moved his practice to North Carolina. My next therapist was concerned about my drinking, but he gave me Stelazine, a very potent antianxiety drug that they give to people who are institutionalized. I was now on a major tranquilizer but still drinking, a combination that could have led to disaster. I was supposed to take Stelazine twice a day, but I reasoned that if I took half of the first dose and skipped the second, I could still drink. I was really playing with fire. Compounding the problem was the fact that although I was depressed, I didn't necessarily see it as depression; I thought I was just neurotic. In reality, I was deeply depressed, and of course alcohol just depresses you further.

Deep depression became the norm of my daily existence. I wasn't working, and I slept a lot. I would get up and get Adam off to school and then go back to bed and sleep the day away. I would set the alarm so that I'd be sure to be awake when Adam came home from school. I didn't want him to think I'd been in bed all day, but I wasn't capable of doing much of anything. I was running out of money, but I also could not push myself or muster the energy necessary to obtain work, let alone deliver the goods onstage. This state of affairs is hard for people to understand and now when I talk about it it's even hard for *me* to absorb, but that's who I was in the early 1970s.

I sold the co-op apartment fairly quickly for $45,000. After the lawyer obtained his percentage, and by the time I had paid all of the closing costs as well as my very large stack of bills, I ended up with about $15,000 to my name. I can still remember the awful sinking feeling of not bringing in any money and watching that $15,000 dribble away, week by week, month after month. Terrifying.

I moved to a rental apartment, and, with no work, I borrowed whatever I could from friends. One awful afternoon there was a strong, repeated knocking at the door. I knew what the knocking signaled: I was months behind on my rent, and the super and the owner were at my door. I asked Adam to be very quiet. I told myself that if they thought I wasn't in they would go away. There was a moment's silence and then I heard their key in the lock. The door opened and there I stood. It was horrible and humiliating.

Adam, age thirteen, decided he had had enough of me and wanted to live full-time with his father. I was devastated. It was absolutely the right thing for Adam to do, but of course I didn't see it that way at the time. On one level it was obvious even to me that my life was a complete mess, but Adam was the only steady thing in my life, and I couldn't bear the thought of losing him. I was horrible to him: "How can you? How can you desert me? Did you know I have something in my mouth and it could be cancer?" This was terrible of me—there is no other word for it—but I couldn't stop. I was desperate. When he left I remember sitting on the edge of my bed, holding myself and rocking. Crying endlessly. The tears just wouldn't stop. I was utterly adrift and drowning in an alcoholic depression.

In oh so many ways my life was a disaster. I was in my forties and had gained a tremendous amount of weight. It was not a pretty picture, but I certainly never thought I was going to die, which made me even more furious when David told Adam, "I think your mother's going to die soon." (I should never have said to Adam that I might have cancer; in fact the bump in my mouth was just that—a bump. I still have it forty years later.) Adam actually has a slightly different recollection, one in which David never used the word "die," but even if he didn't, that was the gist of his remark. I emphasized to Adam: "Please do not worry about this. I am going to be okay. Do not worry about this." I just wanted to reassure my son.

David was now completely in charge, and he ran with the power. I had no financial input into Adam's life, and when it came time for him to choose a college I was not included in the decision at all. There was no discussion whatsoever. I actually don't think Adam had much to say about it himself. David decided he wanted Adam to go to a private school, specifically USC, which David himself had wanted to attend. I think his mind was set in this direction because that's what David had dreamt of when he was a kid.

Once Adam was no longer an adolescent I hardly saw David at all. We would occasionally argue about something on the phone, but that was it. He had married again, a very nice woman named Beth. She and I became friends, a relationship which has continued to this day. She told me that she eventually left David for exactly the same reasons that I had. He just could not abide change and had to control everything; she told me that a week or so after they were married he declared: "You must never invite anyone to the house whom I don't know or who doesn't know my work."

Beth was very kind to Adam. She helped him a lot, and when David gave their son Jacob a dirt bike, but Adam only a book, Beth was furious on Adam's behalf. After their divorce, Beth received a certain amount of money for her share of the house, so she had a bit of financial wherewithal, though certainly not a lot. She promised Adam part of the money she would be receiving from the divorce, and she did in fact give money to him, even though her resources remained limited. Who could have predicted that turn of events? My ex-husband's second wife, now divorced from him, was helping my son with money. It was another lesson in how complicated, and how amazing, people can be—and a lesson in how stupid it is to try to put anyone in a box. Beth is an extraordinarily decent woman, and even though she and David divorced, she promised him that she'd be there when he died. It was a promise she kept, and when his time came, Beth stayed by his side, sleeping on the floor right by his bed until he passed away.

We can't ever fully know another person, no matter how close we are to them or how much we love them. I was about to learn this lesson in spades with my new musical director/arranger/accompanist and very close friend, the brilliant Wally Harper. Wally was about to change my life for the better. I just had to hit absolute rock bottom before that could happen.

I RETAIN ABSOLUTELY no recollection of the very first time Wally and I met, a fact which made both of us laugh throughout our years together. Wally had done summer stock with Joan Kobin, my voice teacher Bob Kobin's wife, and one day when they were talking, Wally said, out of the blue, "I really admire the singing of Barbara Cook." Joan said, "My husband is her teacher"; and when Wally came back to town he met Bob. They shared an instant rapport, and Bob became a kind of surrogate father to him.

Wally and I were both also very friendly with Joan, a delightful, very feminine woman whom men adored. One night she and I were at the opera, and Joan was wearing a beautiful dark-red velvet dress. After the interval, when people were returning to their seats, a gentleman stopped in front of her, admired her dress, and said, "I've been falling into you all evening." Ooh-la-la!

Bob taught his method to Wally, which proved to be a big advantage when we planned and performed our concerts. Thanks to Bob, Wally understood exactly how I sang, and our musical partnership evolved into a shorthand that was closer to musical telepathy. He knew where I was headed both musically and lyrically, and was able to provide the musical underpinnings that gave me both freedom and security onstage. Bob died far too young, suffering a fatal heart attack at only forty-eight, but his work lived on through

Joan, who continued to teach until she died several decades later. I miss them both terribly.

As to that first meeting with Wally, when I was in *She Loves Me*, Bob came to see me backstage and brought Wally with him; Bob introduced us but I have absolutely no memory of meeting Wally. Then, sometime after that encounter Wally wrote a musical, *The Ballad of Romeo and Juliet*, with his then partner Paul Zakrzewski, and they wanted me to play the nurse. They sent me a script and I went to Wally's apartment to discuss it. I decided I didn't want to do the show, but we met again in the summer of 1973, when I was appearing in *The Gershwin Years*. Wally came to see the show three or four times, but for some reason I didn't connect the person visiting backstage with the Wally Harper who had written the *Romeo and Juliet* musical. I really didn't make the connection until I was moving from one apartment to another and came across the script by Paul Zakrzewski and Wally Harper. Finally the lightbulb went on. Of course I was aware of Wally's work on Broadway as a dance arranger on *Company*, and as a composer (he wrote new songs for the Debbie Reynolds show *Irene*), but I had never done any work with him.

By now I hadn't sung in New York for several years and the fellow who was our advance man on *The Gershwin Years* decided he wanted to present me in a solo concert. I had been told by Nancy Dussault that Wally was absolutely the best accompanist around, so people got us together. It's not like I expected an instantaneous meeting of the minds, because everyone has different tastes, but I thought to myself, "What the heck. Let's just see how this turns out." And so, on a cold, wintry day in February of 1974 I went to Wally's apartment on West Seventy-ninth Street to begin working. I walked into his little penthouse carrying the first daffodils of the season, feeling nervous because I didn't know what to expect.

With the thought of that concert (which never came to pass) in our brains, Wally and I began talking, a conversation that never really stopped for the next thirty years. We'd work on songs and then spend hours talking and getting to know each other. Wally was fourteen years younger than I, born in Ohio in 1941. It turned out that his mother was a music teacher who helped to foster his interest in music, particularly a love of the piano, which took hold of him when he was still a small child.

On that first day together we stood in his kitchen, talking about our lives and about music, and even at that first meeting, Wally already had some extraordinary ideas about arranging for me. Ours was a true musical match because our musical sensibilities dovetailed perfectly.

I think the fact that Wally had studied at Juilliard and the New England Conservatory and loved classical music helped put our relationship on a very solid footing. I've always loved classical music, a fact that has informed a lot of my work and phrasing. When, years later, we performed "Not While I'm Around," the Sondheim song from *Sweeney Todd*, there's a point after the bridge when you go back to the melody, and it really kicks in then—it should feel symphonic at that point. It worked like gangbusters when Wally and I performed the song because we both intuitively understood that moment: it's big because it's a sudden broadening. There's no way you're going to understand that unless you have classical music in your ear and in your DNA, and Wally had it in spades.

When I met Wally, he rescued me professionally, plain and simple—that's not too strong a word. I was still at a terrible place in my life and had been forced to give up my apartment and use a friend's place. I was so broke that I was stealing food from the supermarket by slipping sandwich meat in my coat pocket. It was such a terrible moment in my life—I would have been starving if I hadn't stolen from the store. I wasn't shoplifting often, but the fact remains that I did when I was desperate. I had let my appearance go and was wearing patched clothes—in every way I was a mess.

But then I met Wally and things just started to fall into place. In the spring of 1974 we did one evening at the Eugene O'Neill Center in Connecticut. It was the first time we performed together. I was very nervous, exceedingly so, but the response was everything we had hoped for. Then the owner of a little club on Forty-sixth Street in Manhattan, Brothers and Sisters, heard we had gotten some material together and asked us to play the club for a couple of weeks. The response was amazing and the cabaret world now opened up, providing me with a completely new experience: when I had been in a Broadway show I never felt that people were coming to see me—they were coming to see the show. I was therefore genuinely surprised when, at Brothers and Sisters, people reached out to touch me as I walked through the crowd and down the narrow aisle to the stage. We were a big hit, our engagement was extended; and one night, Merle Hubbard, who worked with Herbert Breslin, came to see us.

Herbert was a personal manager and publicist for classical artists. He's the man who was responsible for making Luciano Pavarotti a household name, and he brought Alicia de Larrocha, the pianist, to this country for the first time. Merle insisted Herbert come see us, and although Herbert had never handled a nonclassical singer before, he loved our show and decided he wanted to present us in concert at Carnegie Hall! It was more than a little surreal. The plan was: we were to go from Brothers and Sisters to two weeks at a club in Philadelphia, and then—Holy Hannah!—to Carnegie Hall.

I had played Carnegie Hall, but never as a solo artist. My previous experience at the hall had been as part of a one-night gala in 1961 for Leonard Bernstein's birthday, a benefit for the New York Philharmonic. The first half of that evening was Lenny's classical music, and the second half featured his Broadway material. It was the first time I sang "Glitter and Be Gay" since *Candide* had closed, five years earlier. The applause was thunderous, and I was not only thrilled, but also frightened, and rushed offstage at the end of the song. What happened is that the audience was not only applauding, but also stamping their feet in approval, and the vibration I felt on the stage was so intense that, ridiculous as it sounds, I thought we were having an earthquake. When I made it to the wings I yelled, "What's wrong? What's wrong?" The answer: "Nothing, get back out there!" I was in Carnegie Hall with the New York Philharmonic, singing "Glitter and Be Gay." So so thrilling! But to counteract any nerves, I just kept telling myself I was in Indianapolis.

Well, that evening in honor of Lenny's birthday had occurred thirteen years previously, and headlining my own concert at Carnegie was a completely different affair. I was embarrassed by how much weight I had gained, and I was also terrified. Never in my wildest dreams back in Atlanta had I dreamt of appearing in a solo concert at Carnegie Hall. Never. And to top it off, not only was this my first-ever big solo concert, but it was also being recorded by Columbia Records.

I was still eating too much and I weighed more than I ever had in my life. My drinking was also still a problem. I was feeling pretty lousy about myself and so I shilly-shallied for weeks about committing to Carnegie Hall, just too scared to say, "Yes, let's do it." Breslin's assistant, Merle, called one day and said, "Barbara, to-day's the day. Yes or no. If we don't give Carnegie an answer today we lose the hall." I paused—everything stopped dead. My heart was pounding, and forty years later I can still visualize the little room I was standing in, the pale light coming in through the apartment's only window, the feel of the phone in my sweaty hand . . .

And then, in that moment, as Merle was waiting for my answer, I suddenly saw the whole issue in terms of life and death. "Yes" led toward life. When I saw the situation in those terms my answer became an obvious one. "Yes—I'll do it!" And, to be completely honest, it's not as if I had a real choice: I hadn't sung in New York in quite a while until Brothers and Sisters, hadn't performed much of anywhere in years, and as a result I was nearly flat broke. It was now or never. January 26, 1975, it would be.

Herbert had many connections at Carnegie Hall, and knowing how frightened I was, he did everything he could to help us out. He arranged for Wally and me to walk onto the stage several times so that I could get used to the idea of standing center stage at Carnegie Hall. By this time I had already learned that Wally could be a very funny guy with a sense of humor that was . . . out there. *Waaaaay* out there. And the Carnegie Hall concert just happened to come up when he was in his furniture-licking period. Yes, furniture. If we were in somebody's apartment and the owner was nearby, he would lick the furniture behind their back to make me laugh. So it wasn't really a surprise for me the first time we were allowed onto the Carnegie Hall stage and I saw Wally on his hands and knees, licking the stage of Carnegie Hall.

I think Wally must have been nervous too, but he would never have let it be known. Nerves and all, I was in great spirits; I thought I was singing well, which made me think about the concert with eagerness. I couldn't wait to show off the songs we had planned. My one hesitation was that I still wasn't sure I could make the evening "happen." Could I carry an evening on my own, without the support of a big show? I remember waiting in the wings, and the thrill of having fourteen musicians with me, all in tails. The first violinist turned to the other musicians and said, "Gentlemen—we will walk out together with decorum. This is Carnegie Hall." They walked onstage, I made my entrance, the applause was deafening, and I was on my way.

I hold great memories of that night in January of 1975, starting with the fact that my mother was in attendance. Adam, at age fifteen, was wearing tails, and we hired a limousine so that he could escort his grandmother to the concert in grand style. Even though she was already ill with emphysema and asked to be seated in the last row in case she had a coughing fit and had to leave, she made the effort. I feel so blessed that she saw that triumphant evening. She had been so worried about me—the drinking, the lack of work and money—and now she was present for my triumph. She died one year later.

In February of 1977, one year after my mother's death, I played a week in Atlanta, and while there I felt I should see as much of the family as I could. I invited a lot of them to a get-together at my hotel, and, naturally, my mother was one of the big topics of conversation. I wish I could say that the laughter flowed and that everyone related favorite anecdotes about her, but the truth is that at one point her sister Evelyn and I were reminiscing, and Evelyn said very quietly and gently—"You know, Barbara, Nell could be really mean." Evelyn was right. My mother could be fun—she'd do silly things like put on a hula skirt and dance her Georgia version of a Hawaiian hula—but, sad to say, there was not one single important person in my mother's life that she truly got along with. Not her husband, not her siblings, not even her child.

That great night at Carnegie Hall proved to be the springboard leading to thirty-one years of Wally and me working together, a partnership that changed my life in so many ways. He was a supremely talented man, and every song we performed was very carefully worked out. Because we worked so closely together he always knew exactly where I wanted to go emotionally at each moment in a song, and he always led me there gracefully. Wally's work was enormously sensitive, but lively and swinging when it needed to be.

He found ways to end songs in style, a feat that is surprisingly difficult to pull off. Most people repeat the last line three times, throw in a high ending, and that's it. Wally almost always found new ways to deal with the endings of songs, and our work was all the better for his efforts. I listen now to our recording of "Make the Man Love Me" on my Dorothy Fields tribute CD, *Close as Pages in a Book*, and while I think I sing the song well, what I'm really listening to is Wally's accompaniment. Brilliant. Flawless!

The great part of the Carnegie Hall evening was my finding out that I could hold an entire concert together. I wasn't just singing a bunch of songs—I was making an event of the evening. I felt elated when Herb Breslin came backstage afterward and said, "Barbara, you are a great concert artist."

The live recording sold well, but of course when I listen to it now I hear a lot of the very same mistakes I correct in the young people I work with. I didn't take enough time, rushed through notes and phrases, and during the patter I seemed to be speed-talking through my thoughts. It all rushed by so fast that the subtext seems to be: "I don't want anybody to get bored, so I'll just keep things going." That said, forty years after the recording was made, it's funny—and nice—to hear how spontaneously I related to the audience. I was providing the glue between the songs by means of my patter. I told little stories about how much I loved Jeanette MacDonald and Nelson Eddy. And, heavens! When I was introducing Wally, I started by talking about his love of crossword puzzles, and then I said, "The puzzle was hard today. Did anybody get the clue . . ." And I got so involved in the crossword puzzle that I forgot to say Wally's name, and I never really did introduce him. Terrible.

I listen to "He Was Too Good to Me" on that Carnegie Hall recording, and it's fine, but there's a problem: not only was the key too high, but over the years I also began to sing the song much better, with greater depth of feeling. I know that I can't sing like I sang ten years ago, or even five years ago, but without consciously doing so I have begun to compensate in other ways. I probe more deeply into the lyric and now have a lot more courage to keep going, deeper and deeper.

That entire concert held huge importance for me, not just because it marked my first major reappearance in New York City, but also because it was Carnegie Hall. That's the top of the line and you don't want to mess up. You sure as hell don't want to forget the words, which is something I worry about all the time now. I think if I could have a teleprompter it would take a thousand pounds of worry off my back. The really funny thing is that a reviewer once wrote about me, "It's awful that an artist of Miss Cook's stature would stoop to pretending to forget her lyrics." Pretending?! Who the hell would do that? I've never ever gotten in touch with critics to discuss what they've written about me, but that time I really wanted to.

The Carnegie Hall concert garnered great reviews in the *New York Times* and other major New York press outlets, and led to my playing the concert hall at the Kennedy Center. Another big step. Another great response. Major press. I was in *Time* and *Newsweek* once again. The "C" word started to be used—comeback. The Kennedy Center led to the Dorothy Chandler Pavilion in Los Angeles and then to the Hollywood Bowl. Big, big venues.

Now, that sounds like it was one triumph after another, but it was still a very hard road. In the beginning there was so little money that Wally and I would have to share a hotel room. In the small clubs I'd be getting dressed in the coat room. We worked like hell to make our way up the ladder.

Audiences who remembered me from *The Music Man* and *She Loves Me* were adjusting to the fact that I had gained a good deal of weight during the intervening years. My weight had always been an issue for me. Ironically, though, until I was fifteen I was quite slim; as a child I was anemic, which is what led me to tap-dancing classes. Somehow when I was fifteen I started gaining weight, and I have a feeling it had to do with beginning to menstruate and becoming a woman. Or, to phrase it in another way, becoming a woman and not liking the idea very much; it was as if I wanted to put some distance between me and the world. That distance turned out to be fat.

Why? Well my mother certainly didn't give me a very good picture of becoming a woman. The message was twofold: "This period you get once a month can be painful. And—look out for men, they're no damn good."

The weight I had gained at the time of the Carnegie Hall concert was a recent development. It's not like I had put on too much weight as a teenager; by the time I came to New York I was twenty and chubby, but I weighed no more than 130 pounds—about fifteen pounds overweight. I've got small bones; a really good weight for me was somewhere between 115 and 120.

When weight becomes a concern, however, it colors everything in your life. I had landed in New York, where beautiful thin women seemed to sprout up on every block (and it's even worse in Los Angeles, where the concern with body image can be overwhelming). To this day I can actually remember what I weighed almost every moment of my life. I weighed 136 pounds when I landed the job in *Flahooley*, and that's when I was introduced to Dexedrine (and also Dexamyl) by a weight-loss doctor. It was wonderful in some ways, but of course ultimately terrible in others. Take that little pill and your creative juices can really flow—you feel ready to take on the world with your creativity. You can have all the energy in the world, but there was just one slight problem—the pill was terrible for your overall health, and the damn thing was addictive.

Actually, it was after I took Dexedrine that I really got my weight down. By the time I got married, in March 1952, I weighed 106. I was slim, got rid of the cellulite, and looked terrific, if I do say so myself. However, after all the years of drinking, by the time I really began singing again in the 1970s, my weight had shot way up.

The problem lay in the fact that eating had become inextricably linked with every event in my life. If something good happened, I ate. If something bad happened, I ate. As happens with so many people, I used food as a mood leveler. Food makes you feel okay— for the moment. Then, after you get on a scale, you want to shoot yourself.

There is no question but that there is a genetic component to weight issues. My mother always had to watch her weight. My father was overweight, as were both of my grandmothers. It's easy to forget the genetic aspect, because for people who don't have weight issues, they often simply view overweight people as gluttons.

When I was performing in all those Broadway musicals I was able to stay at a good weight because I felt I had to—I wouldn't have had a career if I weren't careful. But—when I started drinking so heavily my weight shot up. Alcohol contains a huge number of calories, and to compound the problem I was also not getting any exercise. Add in my concurrent depression and all of the pieces were in place for a big weight gain.

I was huge by the time of the Carnegie Hall concert in 1975, and I started to feel like that was all anyone was talking about. Despite those great reviews of the concert, even the *New York Times* ran contrasting photos of me—one when I was slender, and one after all the weight gain. I would go on television talk shows and the hosts didn't want to talk about music—they wanted to talk about weight.

Did the weight issues affect my career at the time? Probably, but I'll never know for certain. I do know that Fred de Cordova, the producer of Johnny Carson's *Tonight Show*, did not want fat white women on his show. In other words, forget the talent—he didn't want that look on his show.

Over the years my weight has continued to yo-yo. Of course I'd like to weigh less than I do, and I'm working at it. I eat the same healthy foods on a daily basis. I can't move easily now, so it is much more difficult for me to lose weight. I've been able to keep off the fifty pounds I dropped from my Carnegie Hall weight, and the fact that I don't drink has certainly helped. I haven't completely solved my weight issues, but I'm better. I guess I remain a work in progress.

I've always noticed how much other women weigh—we all do—which led to a very funny incident while I was performing on Broadway in *Sondheim on Sondheim*. One of my costars was Vanessa Williams, and, boy oh boy, does she look terrific. Nearly fifty with an incredible body. Great legs—and, man, does she work at keeping in shape. Anyway, we were onstage singing "Waiting for the Girls Upstairs," and she and I were sitting stage left on a little bench. She had a kind of low-cut dress on and I just happened to notice her décolletage. She's so beautiful, and in a completely non-sexual way I was looking and admiring her cleavage—and forgot to sing part of the song! I was checking out Vanessa's breasts and I forgot to sing.

After the Carnegie Hall concert, I began working my way up the ladder and played a small hot club in New York City called Reno Sweeney (named after the lead character in Cole Porter's *Anything Goes*). In order to generate publicity, my manager at the time decided that we should have "celebrity night" on Mondays and Tuesdays, in hopes that their appearances would generate column mentions. I remember that James Beard came one night, but the truth is that we ran out of celebrities pretty quickly. And that is when Lillian Hellman reentered my life. That was one of the great things about Lillian—she showed up. She had terrible emphysema by then and leaned heavily on the arm of her escort, but by God, she came. And very put-together. She didn't have to show up, but she did. After the show, she came back to the crowded little office that served as my dressing room. She asked me if she could smoke. Most of the time I said no to people, but I just couldn't say no to her. What an incongruous sight. Lillian Hellman in that stupid little room where I changed my clothes and had to do my makeup. I was so moved that she had come to be there for me.

I know Mary McCarthy hated Lillian and said that every word she wrote was a lie, including "a", "and", and "the", but that's not the Lillian I knew. Not only did I admire her writing—it just flows, you never see the effort—but I loved her spirit. During that time in the 1950s when a lot of very respectable people like Jerry Robbins were not behaving honorably, Lillian put herself on the line in a very public fashion: "I cannot and will not cut my conscience to fit this year's fashions" was her defiant reply to the HUAC. What a beautiful and powerful statement in the midst of a very difficult time.

When, after Carnegie Hall, I really started working in earnest, Herb Breslin was managing me. Unfortunately we were just not a good fit. He was a classical music guy and I was now a cabaret and concert performer. I realized that Wally was not going to help me out of this jam with Herb because Wally was the least confrontational person in the world. His way of handling any problem was to just walk away. He couldn't handle the discord. He'd never get angry with anyone—except the people to whom he was really close. Instead, he would just up and leave. In this case, I was with Wally at Herb's office, and Herb kept saying, "Are you going to sign for films?"

"No."

"Are you going to sign for concerts?"

"No."

I said no to every single proposal, until I finally said, "Herbert, I'm sorry. It's just that we come from two different worlds, and I think it's not going to work." He was devastated and didn't speak to me for years. Some time later we finally made up and repaired our relationship. At the time, however, he was furious and the relationship was totally ruptured. But I had to trust my instincts, and I just knew it was all wrong for me; I remember that Herbert had ne-gotiated a recording deal that promised something like $5,000, and Aaron Russo, Bette Midler's manager at the time, took over and negotiated a deal for me that was five times as large: $25,000. But in telling Herb that our business relationship wasn't going to work, the real life lesson for me was that I found myself being the strong one and standing up for myself. Once again, it wasn't the men who stood tall. Wally sat silently while I told Herbert it was over.

I now realize that this has been a recurring motif in my life: women of my generation generally married and were taken care of, but I never fit that pattern. When I was growing up in Atlanta, a young girl felt she had to make a good marriage—that that was the most important thing she needed to accomplish. Women often didn't work outside the home and they typically depended on a man for their security. I, on the other hand, have never depended on a man financially. Never. I think there is a lot to be said for women who have learned to take care of themselves.

Conversely, I did depend on men emotionally—very much so. This was the case with both my husband and with Wally, and although I was stronger than both of them, I didn't realize it at the time. Nowadays I fully realize that I can take care of myself, because I did so through some very bad times and still emerged intact. Even during my darkest days with alcohol, when I just couldn't stop drinking, I absolutely knew somewhere deep inside me that I would be okay.

As I started working in better venues, Arthur Cantor handled publicity for me, but things really took off in 1979, when I joined forces with Jerry Kravat, who began to serve as my personal man-ager. Arthur had been doubling as my manager, but Jerry now wanted to fill that position, and I spent quite a bit of time mulling this question over. I'm a cautious person, and I wasn't sure it was the right thing to do. But—it sounded right, and Wally and I agreed to give it a try. For a while that meant paying two separate commissions to two different managers. That lasted through several gigs, but then Jerry took over the managerial role completely, and brought my career to an entirely different level.

The problem remained, however, that even after the Carnegie Hall and Kennedy Center triumphs, I was still drinking. My mother had died after a long and difficult illness, and that illness had only exacerbated my own problems: the sicker she became, the more I ate and drank. The net result was that I became sicker as well. I knew I was on a terrible downward track but I simply couldn't seem to gain any control over it. Everything was falling apart.

In February of 1977 I was in Los Angeles, playing a club called the Back Lot, when my body decided it wasn't going to take it anymore. I was in such bad shape that just shampooing my hair before the show took all my energy. I'd shampoo and then have to lean against the shower wall to get my energy back. By the time I was ready for the show I was exhausted. Compounding the problem was the demanding schedule: I was working six nights a week, two shows per night. That's twelve shows per week for two weeks, a total of twenty-four shows. I think of the twenty-four scheduled shows, I only made something like fifteen. I canceled the rest because I just couldn't do it. The capper came when, with two more days to go on the gig, I had a major panic attack. I thought I was dying, because that's how I always felt with a major panic attack. I was debilitated after nearly ten years of heavy drinking, and my body was saying "no more."

As the panic attack fully blossomed, Wally put me in the car and we tore off to the emergency room at ninety miles per hour. They gave me a tranquilizer and said I was not having a heart attack, but rather, a major panic attack. Heart attack or not, I was really frightened. The doctor I saw also mentioned the possibility of adrenal gland cancer, and I froze, but he wasn't through: "You're very close to diabetes. Your body is shutting down. You have to stop drinking. Now."

I knew I was in big physical trouble, but my immediate response to the doctor's command was a simple "I don't think I can." Even then I still didn't believe I had a drinking problem. I had a "calorie" problem and just couldn't stop eating and drinking. I knew the problem meant that with my body betraying me I couldn't work, and that as a result the most essential part of my identity was being taken away—yet the drinking continued.

It was an awful, awful time. With the club date over I was still in L.A., spending most of my time in bed, having panic attacks. My friend George Connolly let Wally and me stay in his house. He would sit by the bed for hours, not talking, simply holding my hand. He's still a close friend—a very good man.

When I finally got back to New York, a physician I knew put me on a strict low-carbohydrate, high-protein regimen, which was then the best-known treatment for hypoglycemia, the diagnosis I had been given in L.A. I was able to stick to this new way of eating, and for a while I was able to stay away from alcohol. I began to lose some of my excess weight and my head began to clear.

The most astounding things had begun to occur: I was getting my life back—I had stopped drinking and the terrible depression and great heaviness that had descended on me every morning were gone. Gone! It was as if someone had opened a window and let the sunshine and light and playfulness back in. For the first time in years I was able to plan little pleasures and look forward to them with great joy. What a wonderfully silly Thanksgiving I had that year. Wally and I were working in Washington and decorated our hotel suite with garlands of paper leaves, as well as paper turkeys with those fanlike tails. I even bought little cardboard Pilgrims to mark each place at the table, and our friend Jonathan Hadary made Pilgrim hats with aluminum-foil buckles. I'm sure there must have been more worthwhile things to do with one's sobriety, but at the time this all looked mighty good to me.

Now, to what exactly do you suppose I attributed all this great change? Why, it was the result of my new low-carb, high-protein diet, of course. Everything was clicking into place. I had even stopped drinking, so as far as I was concerned that sad old chapter in my life was finished.

Which leads to one overwhelming conclusion: it is impossible to overstate the power of denial. As I shall demonstrate . . .

Wally and I had just finished a second studio album for Columbia and I was out celebrating with my colleagues. They were drinking Champagne and I was toasting with my Perrier. And then on the way home, I thought to myself, "Screw this. I'm gonna celebrate too!" So I stopped to buy a half gallon of my old favorite, Gallo Chablis. I hadn't had anything to drink for about six months, so it won't surprise anyone to know that it didn't take me long to get very drunk. I drank at least half of that big jug of wine and fell asleep—passed out is more like it.

I woke up about four hours later, in the middle of another terrifying panic attack. For the first time ever I made the association of the panic attacks with drinking. When the panic subsided, I looked at the half-filled glass of wine by my bed and said, "I am never going to do that again." And I knew, in every cell of my body, that I'd stick to that vow. Nearly forty years have passed since that moment and I have not touched a drop of alcohol since. The desire has vanished.

Even when the album that was the occasion of that final celebration with wine didn't do well, I didn't resume drinking. The album, titled *As of Today*, represented my one attempt at a pop record. The problem lay in the fact that the combination of that musical idiom and my theatrical soprano voice just didn't work. There are some good things on the recording, most notably a beautiful Janis Ian song called "Stars." We mixed in a few standards, like Irving Berlin's "What'll I Do," but the end result was neither fish nor fowl. I actually had known we were in big trouble as soon as we brought the recording to the Columbia Records executive who was to sign off on the finished product. He hated the record. Really hated it. It was clear that there would be no big promotional push and that the record was not going to go anywhere.

Completely sober, I began to work nonstop and eventually began attending a 12-step program—it just took me ten years after I stopped drinking to get there. I didn't want to go for a long time because I didn't want to call myself an alcoholic. I thought, "I've stopped. What the hell do you want? Fuck off!" I think what changed my mind is that at this same time I also began to grapple with my food addiction and was attending a 12-step group for eating disorders. I had tried this program some years before and had given up on it. But by 1987, when I put together my Broadway show *A Concert for the Theatre*, I was unhappy with my weight gain, and my son, Adam, said to me: "Why don't you go back to the meetings for food addiction?" I started attending those meetings, and after about one week I thought to myself, "This is about bone-crunching honesty. And that means I have to get honest about my drinking, too." I was ten years sober at the time, but I knew I needed to attend the meetings. I promised myself I would give it five years. It was one of the smartest decisions I've ever made.

It was not easy for me to get there. The first time I went I was alone. I opened the door and looked into what felt like the brightest room I had ever seen, when suddenly all the heads in the room turned and were staring at me. I closed the door and walked away. I was rescued by two friends who knew the rooms very well. They held my hands and walked me into my first meeting a few days later.

I discovered a truly beautiful fellowship. I stuck around and met some great people, all recovering alcoholics like me. They have given me tools that help me get through the day a little more easily. And one of the great things is that no matter where I am in the world, I know there are rooms I can go to and be welcomed and understood.

For all their similarities, however, there is a substantial difference between food- and alcohol-addiction programs: if your problem is with alcohol, you know—theoretically, at least—that you can turn your back on it. You don't have to drink in order to live. If your addiction is to food, however, there is no getting around the fact that you have to eat. You have to walk the tiger three times every day.

I had trouble with the "higher power" concept, but the program helped me with my search for a deeper spirituality. I would bring needlepoint to the meetings, sit and listen, and eventually came to realize that the meetings were helping me become a more honest person. They help you lead a more moral life, teaching you to follow through on your commitments. Don't say "yes" if you don't mean "yes." Show up. Be present. Moment by moment, day by day, I learned to sometimes "let it go." There are no hard-and-fast rules in this program, but rather suggestions to help you lead a better life. The program helped me to calm down, and it definitely helped me connect with my audiences in an easier and more grounded manner. Gone were the days of excessive nervousness about speaking, because once I had shared at a number of meetings, I was no longer nervous talking to my audience between songs. Now I wanted to connect with the audience through my stories as well as my songs.

I believe my sobriety is a gift. I don't take credit for it. Was a higher power at work? I don't know. I was scared that my body was shutting down and I still wanted to live, and work, and love. After looking at that half-filled glass by my bedside I somehow knew I would never, ever, take a drink again.

I also know that some people just can't do it—they cannot and will not stop drinking, and refuse to join a program. I think about a friend who died in 2001. She was a terrific person who simply refused to stop drinking. I had organized an intervention for her in November of 1987 because by that time she had spent the previous ten months in bed, recovering, she said, from an injury to her leg. Finally it got through to me: nine or ten months in bed seemed excessive. Then when she asked me once again to lend her money—which she always paid back—Adam said I must stop enabling her. He was right, of course. I had taken her to one 12-step meeting with me, but that was all I had been able to accomplish—hence the intervention.

During this intervention, close friends reminded her of some of the dreadful drunken things she had done. Passing out at the dinner table. Peeing on herself and lying on the floor in her urine. Having to be cleaned up, carried upstairs, and put to bed. Passing out in a restaurant with her face falling forward into her plate, the owner of the restaurant saying she was not welcome to return. I kept thinking, "This could have been me."

She heard everything that was said, but couldn't and wouldn't take it in. Whenever we talked about her drinking, she said she could stop anytime she wanted to—she just didn't want to. Boy, that's an old one. She had run a successful PR business, representing major celebrities and public figures. Now she just stayed home and drank.

We had known each other for over thirty years and she had declared herself Adam's godmother. I loved her. But after the intervention we never had anything to do with each other again. I tried. I called to see how she was. I said I loved her and wanted to help her but she wasn't interested. Finally I stopped calling.

And then, in 2001, she was dead—from cancer and alcoholism. When I first heard the news I wondered if I had done the right thing with the intervention. Was there an intermediate step I should have taken first? What might I have done differently? Fifteen years later I'm certain none of it would have made any difference.

When I heard that she was dead I couldn't stop crying. Did I survive because of some genetic luck of the draw? I don't know. She threw her life away, and somehow I was saved from that same fate. Another friend told me that there were no plans for any kind of a memorial gathering or service. No getting together to talk about the fun times. I just can't bear to think of that. It seems so brutal.

When you read about Bill W.'s journey to sobriety, he says that some higher power struck him to the floor. I'm not a big believer in organized religion—I think an overwhelming amount of harm has been done in the name of religion. I know some of the following is hard to believe, but Anthony Hopkins, an acquaintance who has been very kind to me, talks about a similar thing—of being struck—"Boom! And it was over. It was like a great pilot light was lit"—and from that moment on not drinking. It's odd, and hard to explain. When somebody asks me, "How did you stop drinking?" I don't have much of an answer for them. I didn't do it. It was a gift. I'm not sure exactly where it came from. Part of it was my associating the drinking with the panic attacks. You'll do just about anything to avoid a panic attack. They are horrible and debilitating because they are different from the anxiety and stress that we all live with. An honest-to-God clinical panic attack contains one moment, always, when you're sure you're dying. You think there is no way any human body can go through what you're experiencing and survive.

When the panic attacks happen, you're so overwhelmed by the panic that you can't think clearly. After experiencing several such attacks, however, I realized that I *had* once again survived, so it occurred to me to try to pay attention to the symptoms. "Okay," I'd say to myself, "I have that funny feeling in my scalp. My heart is beating out of my chest. I feel hot. But . . ." Then I would address the symptoms logically, observe and pin them down, and tell myself: "Okay, I've got this. I've got that. It's a panic attack. I'm not going to die. I'm going to get out of it. I will survive." Once I stopped drinking, little by little the attacks went away. Occasionally I would have a tiny wave of one, but eventually they really did disappear.

LOOKING BACK ON my drinking years, there's a hell of a lot I regret. During the years when I should have been doing my best work in the theater I was unemployable. After I stopped drinking, however, I became comfortable in the cabaret and concert worlds, where I could call the shots myself. I finally had control. Wally and I put the shows together and I sang what I wanted.

I recorded album after album, choosing material that spoke directly to me: *The Disney Album*, *It's Better with a Band*, *The Champion Season*, *Live from London*, *Oscar Winners*, the Grammy-nominated Christmas album *Count Your Blessings*. I have appeared on thirty-six recordings besides the nine original cast recordings of shows in which I performed. I've recorded everything from *Songs of Perfect Propriety*, a 1958 album featuring poems by Dorothy Parker with music by Seymour Barab, to albums of songs by Jerome Kern, George Gershwin, and Oscar Hammerstein. Believe me, I know how fortunate I have been and still am to spend my singing life with this great material. I think that as I get older I have even more courage to go deeper and deeper into the text. It makes me think of Nelson Riddle's comment about Sinatra's masterful singing on his torch-song albums like *Only the Lonely*: "Ava taught him how to sing those songs—the hard way."

The transition from being a cast member of a Broadway show to solo artist did not feel like an abrupt change to me. I was really just returning to my roots—my first professional appearance in New York City had been at the Blue Angel nightclub. People had always asked me to sing in intimate settings, especially at parties, so it felt natural to me. I actually felt set free in many ways because I was now in complete control: I chose which songs to sing, what order they should be sung in, and exactly what the patter between songs would be. I was in charge and I relished the opportunity.

My approach to singing didn't change, but I felt that I improved every year. I developed more courage with my emotional choices, digging deeper and deeper into the lyric. Our influences as artists can come from anywhere and everywhere, and I found that even in intimate settings, my love of opera had really deepened my skills as a performer; good opera singers who can also act have to put themselves out on a limb and take chances; watching the opera singers who succeeded at this, who delivered moving and affecting characterizations even within the oftentimes larger-than-life world of opera, inspired me, giving me the courage to make ever bolder choices of my own.

I was invited to sing at the White House for the first time, and make no mistake—performing at the White House is a thrill, no matter what your political affiliations. Besides that first invitation to sing for President Carter, I was fortunate to also sing for the Clintons, George H. W. Bush, and Ronald Reagan. It was singing for the Reagans in April of 1988 that remains most firmly etched in my mind, not only because of Nancy Reagan's kind invitation, but also because of the sad evidence of the president's diminished capacity. The Reagans hosted a rather small (for them) dinner party for the king and queen of Sweden upstairs in their private dining room, and Nancy asked me to come to dinner and then sing for the royals. The evening began with cocktails downstairs, and I happened to be sitting with Helena Shultz, the wife of Secretary of State George Shultz, who told me we were really in for a treat since the dinner was to be upstairs. The Reagans rarely invited people to their private quarters—Helena herself had never been invited up before. There were only about thirty people at four tables. Nancy was sitting right next to the king at one table, while at the table directly across, the queen sat next to President Reagan.

This was during the time when Nancy would often be seen whispering to the president and looking as if she were telling him what to do. Well, as it turns out she was. At the end of the dinner President Reagan got up to make a toast and began, "If Nancy were here I know she'd want me to say . . ." And there she was, only a few feet away, next to the king of Sweden and directly across from the president. I was startled, to say the least. We were then to move into another room, where I would sing. Reagan announced the wrong room, and Nancy gently corrected him, again. Finally, I sang several songs, but before I finished, the president got up to thank me mid-performance, and Nancy said, "Sit down, dear— the lady hasn't finished." "Oh my God!" I thought. "All this can't be happening. He's the president."

What didn't occur to me at the time was how difficult this must have been for Mrs. Reagan. Here's this man, whom she adores, this man who had become the president of the United States, slipping away from her; she was trying to help him, and being put down for it in the press.

I also sang for Queen Elizabeth and Prince Philip at the 1997 Royal Variety performance. After the performance everyone lines up to meet Her Majesty. I was nervous—Helen Mirren calls it "Queenitis—the tendency to babble nonsense"—and I managed the usual "I'm so thrilled to meet you." I then added, "As a little girl I played with my Princess Elizabeth and Princess Margaret paper dolls . . ." The queen smiled and then laughed—a very queenly laugh, I might add. Definitely not a belly laugh. She was gracious, which is not exactly how I would describe Prince Philip after the show. During my performance, before we sang a duet of "People Will Say We're In Love," my vocal partner, Michael Ball, had introduced the song as "Queen Elizabeth and Prince Philip's favorite song when they were courting." That obviously did not sit well with the prince, because after the show, while we stood in the receiving line, he barked, "Who said that was our favorite song? Nonsense!"

Equally exciting was my recent performance for the justices of the Supreme Court. Once a year they have these musical afternoons in a very intimate setting, a beautiful wood-paneled room in the Supreme Court Building with seating for no more than seventy-five or so. Sandra Day O'Connor used to plan these annual events, and now they've been taken over by Justice Ruth Bader Ginsburg, whom I admire enormously. The great John Pizzarelli and I were both asked to perform. John and I have done several concerts together that really worked well, but that afternoon we both sang solo.

While John was on, I peeked out and there in the front row was Clarence Thomas. My heart sank. I'm gonna sing for Clarence Thomas. Clarence Thomas who is famous for never speaking in the Court. Would he sit like a stone statue during my performance? HELP!

I walked on, took my place, and there, directly in front of me, no more than five feet away, was Chief Justice Roberts. And just over to my right, the mute Justice Thomas. But, boy, was I surprised by him. As I was singing he had a huge smile on his face—

loving it. Laughing at every joke, and when I got to my list of funny country-song titles, he nearly fell out of his chair. I don't know what came over me, but I yelled, "Clarence, control yourself!" He laughed even harder. After the show he came over to me and we had a very pleasant time together. He was completely charming. Never, never would I have expected that the Clarence I was enjoying was hidden there inside the political Clarence I knew from the news.

Shortly before I sang for the Reagans, Wally and I had decided that I should return to Broadway, but in concert. Early on, when we first started thinking of a Broadway evening for me, Wally found someone he thought should be our producer. With all of Wally's good qualities, he was often not a good judge of people, and I never felt secure about this proposed producer. Finally, when it was time to sign a contract, I refused. Wally was furious with me. But thank God I didn't sign. We later found out the guy was a crook.

I learned another painful lesson on the show because, although I was nearly sixty years old, I was still too trusting. We had begun to put the show together and some producers were interested, but when I learned that Wally's partner Michael was looking for additional producers for me, I told Wally I didn't want to be represented in any way by Michael. He had good qualities and he could be funny as hell, but he could also be a total pain in the ass and was not always good with people. Wally said, "No problem—he won't be involved. I had a long talk with him last night and it's okay"— but the very next day there was Michael at the production meeting about the show. I was so angry at that meeting I thought I was going to have a stroke. When Wally went to the men's room one of the producers who was already involved picked up on my feelings and said, "Barbara, how do you feel about Michael's participation?" I said, "I don't like it at all. I don't want him to be involved." When Wally came back and found out what I had said he was livid.

The Shuberts eventually came on board as producers and we had the right theater, so it felt like now or never. We opened at the Ambassador Theatre in April of 1987 and called the evening *A Concert for the Theatre*. The show was a big mistake and simply didn't work. We were usually so careful about repertoire, but we really screwed up this time. Frank Rich reviewed it badly in the *Times*, and I think he was right. I received a Drama Desk Award for Outstanding One Person Show but I knew the show should have been better. The timing was off in every way and it proved to be a terrible, terrible time for Wally. Michael, whom he adored, was dying of AIDS. We watched him disappear day by day and then he was gone. Very, very hard stuff. No way to concentrate on putting a show together.

Wally and I patched up our disagreement and continued to work together for another seventeen years. It's a sign of how strong our bond was that in three decades of working together, we never did sign any sort of contract. Back in 1974 we just shook hands on our deal. That deal lasted for all of our thirty-one years together.

Subsequent to *A Concert for the Theatre*, I was singing at the Carlyle Hotel in New York—a beautiful intimate room, very Upper East Side, very elegant and expensive. Stephen Holden wrote in his review: "She's not singing the sort of material that suits her best." And of course he was right. From then on, there would be no more attempts at pop singing. Leave those songs to Lena. Theater songs and what is now known as The Great American Songbook—Gershwin, Porter, Berlin, and Kern—was the music that really suited me.

Concert jobs started to flow my way. I was singing not just with Wally but with beautiful symphony orchestras that he conducted. Whatever the musical setting, it seemed to work, mostly because I could sing well. And after everything I had been through, when I was singing a sad song, I knew what I was singing about.

Gone were the days of tiny clubs and changing in shoebox offices. I sang everywhere from London's Royal Albert Hall to the Sydney Opera House. I traveled to China, and one night in Moscow, along with Tommy Tune and Wally, I found myself singing "White Christmas" to Soviet rock musicians. Not only was I earning a very nice income, but my chronic problems with the IRS were finally cleared up. When things had been at their worst I ended up owing the IRS three years' back taxes, a figure that ran into six figures. It scared the hell out of me. I was no spring chicken—how the hell would I be able to pay them and still have money for my old age? But I paid it. I didn't pay it all at once, but I paid it, and after eighteen months I was square with the government.

At the time I was really upset about having to pay the government all that money, and I was crying when I called Adam to complain. But Adam, as usual, put it in perspective for me. He said, "Mom, this is not your money. It never has been. It was never yours in the first place. You've just been holding on to something that doesn't belong to you." Suddenly, all the fear and anger just lifted off my shoulders and vanished. Adam is very good about things like that—he can see the big picture.

He is talented in so many areas, and happens to be very smart about finance. His first big job after college was at Merrill Lynch. When you start at Merrill Lynch you have to make cold calls, and you get hung up on nine times out of ten. Talk about a tough training ground. It was absolutely no fun, but Adam said that the train-ing actually helped prepare him for life's difficulties. He also had a job selling shares of oil in California, a job that landed him a six-figure salary. He also directs shows, and with his love of theater and opera seems to have found where he belongs.

Adam is a really good, honest man, and when he sat me down in 1989 to tell me, "Mom—I'm gay," I laughed. I thought he was joking. He had been living with a lovely young woman for a couple of years and we all thought they'd get married. I was shocked, to say the least. When he said he had something important to tell me, I thought maybe he was going to tell me they were breaking up. We had a long conversation, and then, when he was at the door, about to leave I said, "Oh, Adam, what will I do when you bring somebody home to meet me?" Adam replied, "Don't worry, Mom. It'll be fine. He'll say, 'Oh, Barbara, I just love your work.'" But it just wasn't funny to me. When he left, I started crying—I mean, really sobbing—and except when I was asleep, that crying jag lasted five full days.

Finally I said to myself, "What the hell is going on with you? You've known and worked with gay men your entire career." After my thirty thousand years of working with several different thera-pists, I got out my toolbox and began to try to understand what was happening. As a young person, I had always felt like an outsider—a little girl with her nose pressed against the window, not able to get in. And then having Adam, a man-child, made me feel that I was finally plugged into the mainstream. Somehow, his telling me he was gay had suddenly unplugged me. I had a new son, a new person I didn't fully know. It also occurred to me that I probably wouldn't have grandchildren. That's a hard one. But—the final step for me was when I understood that Adam wasn't here to plug me into any-

thing. I was here to help him be Adam—as fully as possible. That was twenty-five years ago, and I am so happy to say we have a very close, loving relationship.

As my concert career continued to flourish, I kept thinking about returning to Broadway in a full-fledged book musical. But where, I kept asking myself, was the right vehicle?

The answer came in the form of a run of only two nights, but what a two nights it was: a concert version of Stephen Sondheim's legendary musical *Follies,* which was to be recorded by RCA Records. I would play the role of showgirl-turned-housewife Sally Durant Plummer.

The odd thing was that aside from my admiration for Stephen's brilliant score, I had never been a huge fan of *Follies.* When I saw the original Broadway production I just didn't care who went off with whom, because I didn't care about them as people. Ironically, I had auditioned for the role of Sally in the 1971 original Broadway production. My drinking was nowhere near as bad as it would later become and I made a point of looking my best for my audition. I think I actually looked too good: Hal saw *Follies* as a show about people on the downward slide—people past their prime—and I didn't look the part. When I finally did see the show, it just didn't fully work for me on the bottom-line emotional level.

Same thing with *Company.* In fact, it took me a while to fully appreciate just how brilliant *Company* is; the show premiered in 1970 and was so far ahead of its time that my initial reaction was negative—I thought the show was antimarriage and antifamily. Of course I've revised my opinion, even if I still do find some of the characters a little off-putting. In reality, *Company*'s climactic song, "Being Alive," actually affirms the importance of commi'

ment and relationships, but at the time it all struck me as a bit sour. The same thing happened eight years later with *Sweeney Todd*. When I first saw the show I thought, "Why the hell do I have to come to the theater and hear somebody sing that the world is full of shit and we're all swimming around in it?" It took me a while to come around, but I now believe the show is Stephen's masterpiece.

So, when producer Thomas Shepard called Jerry Kravat to ask about my participation in the *Follies* concerts, even though I knew that beautiful score was going to be played by the Philharmonic, I just wasn't sure. Two nights only? A short rehearsal period of something like four days? And I'd never done one of Stephen's shows. But I thought about it, and fortunately I realized that the concerts represented a great opportunity and said yes. This would be Stephen Sondheim, and what's more, it was Sondheim with an incredible cast: Lee Remick, George Hearn, Mandy Patinkin, Phyllis Newman, Liliane Montevecchi, Carol Burnett, and Comden and Green. We all knew each other's histories and had great respect for each other.

Our intense, abbreviated rehearsal period proved to be very exciting. There was so little time that it was scary as hell for all of us. My old friend Herbie Ross was our director. He was terrifically talented as both director and choreographer, and our bond was so strong after those summers at Tamiment that one day when we had a break in rehearsals, we just happened to lock eyes as we sat in that small room at Avery Fisher Hall. It was as if we both simultaneously remembered our history of thirty-five years, wordlessly crossing the room to hug each other while crying. We each knew exactly what the other was thinking. Herb was such an interesting, complex man; his marriage with the brilliantly talented ballerina

Nora Kaye really worked, and yet when I first met him he was in a homosexual relationship. It just goes to show you—human beings don't always fit into neat little boxes.

Stephen had requested that I play Sally, and thank goodness I said yes. His work reminds me of Shakespeare, because, like the Bard, you can revisit his work time and time again and there is always something new to discover. If Stephen knew I compared him to Shakespeare he'd start snorting like a bull and charge at me, but I stand by the comparison. His songs are so rich and full of wisdom that singing one is like being an actress given the opportunity to play a great scene.

None of us had done the show before, and the orchestra was situated behind us, which meant that we could get help from the conductor, Paul Gemignani, only if we turned the microphone sideways so that we were in profile to the audience. But—the concerts worked brilliantly, and those two nights at Avery Fisher Hall proved to be among the most thrilling of my entire career. The audience went wild, the ovations rolling on and on, increasing in volume until the room seemed ready to explode. It simply does not get better than performing Sondheim with an all-star cast and the New York Philharmonic.

I listed our extraordinary *Follies* cast above, but there was also one other cast member of particular note: singing "Broadway Baby" was none other than Elaine Stritch.

Elaine Stritch. A major, major, piece of work. Or, as the *New York Times* described her: "Elaine Stritch, the brassy, tart-tongued Broadway actress and singer."

Elaine was one of the first people I met and admired when I first came to New York. She was in a hit revue at that time, *Angel in the Wings*, and gained notice for the wacky song "Civilization

(Bongo, Bongo, Bongo, I Don't Want to Leave the Congo)." She could be difficult to work with but she was also deeply talented. So most of the time, people were willing to put up with her shenanigans in order to add her talent to the proceedings.

I could write four chapters on Elaine alone, but a few anecdotes will suffice, beginning with *Follies*. It was a glorious experience for all of us, a major event, and there were a lot of big names in that rehearsal room, but Elaine still managed to make herself the center of attention. Check out the DVD of the concert; there I am, in rehearsal, singing the moving "In Buddy's Eyes." Everybody in the room is rapt, but there's Elaine in the background changing her shoes and fixing her clothes. It's like she couldn't stop herself. "Look at me. Look at me."

Elaine was, and remained right up until the end of her life, a force of nature and a big-time talent. I liked her very much but she could also be a major-league pain in the ass, self-centered to the max. I did respect her enormously, and she was a great performer, but boy oh boy could she make me crazy.

When I was singing at Feinstein's at the Regency, a very smart, classy cabaret space on Manhattan's Upper East Side, I had included a very quiet ballad, one that I felt would really mean something to audiences. I came to that moment in the show, the audience was hushed, but right there in the middle of the song was Elaine making this loud rustling, bustling sound in that big shopping bag that never left her side, because she decided she had to give herself an insulin injection in the middle of that number. She just couldn't wait three minutes.

In 1997 I was invited by the Royal Philharmonic Orchestra to join them at the Royal Albert Hall in London in a concert to celebrate my seventieth birthday. I asked three people to join me in that concert: Maria Friedman, Tommy Körberg, who sang brilliantly in the London production of *Chess*, and Elaine.

One very blustery, sleety, awful day, she came to Wally Harper's apartment to rehearse before we went to London. As I said, the weather was horrible that day and when she walked in her hair was in curlers and covered by a shower cap. I just assumed she was going out to dinner later and was protecting her hair. When Wally's little dog jumped up to greet her, she said, commandingly, to the little dog: "Down! I want no love!"

She then barked: "Give me a cuppa coffee, NOW! If I don't get it right now, I'm leaving!" So, she got her coffee and we began rehearsing, and after we'd worked a while, Elaine stopped and announced: "You know what I like about show business? I'll tell you what I like about show business. I walked in here forty-five minutes ago with a shower cap on my head and nobody said a goddamned thing!"

She was a very hard worker. Much more than I am. She would rehearse something for hours in pursuit of perfection. I urged her many, many times to do cabaret. She was terrified. I said, "Elaine, all you have to do is find some songs you like. Go out there and be yourself—sing, talk—you'll be dynamite." She was, of course, a very clever lady and she took my cabaret idea and ran with it. She got all these high-powered folks like writer John Lahr and director George Wolfe to help her put an entire show together—the show that became *Elaine Stritch at Liberty*. It was a smash and we later ended up in competition for the same Tony Award. The joke was on me because I found myself thinking, "Why the hell didn't I keep my mouth shut?!" She deserved the Tony for her beautifully performed show. It was then filmed for HBO and she won an Emmy. Both totally deserved.

Perhaps our most notable joint work experience came when we performed a benefit concert for Lincoln Center Theater. It was, in a word, a nightmare.

Jack O'Brien was directing the evening, and one day he couldn't be at rehearsal. In the director's absence she took over and was so rude to almost everybody in the room that I thought somebody was going to have a stroke, and that included me. I mean that. I decided that she was toxic. It was hazardous to work with her. She made you so angry it was dangerous to your health. I'd known her all those years, and, going into the benefit, I thought we could help raise some money for Lincoln Center Theater, and that the evening would work like gangbusters. I had even thought for a long time that we should organize some concerts together. My manager, Jerry Kravat, thought it was a great idea and that he could book us all over the place. We were so vastly different, and we respected each other's work. I also thought she knew I wasn't afraid of her, which I wasn't. I told myself, "I can deal with her." Well, I was wrong. Big time.

She was extraordinarily difficult to work with because she was extremely overbearing. Although she often had good ideas, she was like a steamroller. She was so impossible that at one point she was actually trying to tell me how to sing a song. I finally said, "For Christ's sake, Elaine, don't try to tell me how to sing the fucking song. I've never sung the fucking song before. I don't know how I want to sing the fucking song. I need to find out—so just leave me the fuck alone!"

Perhaps she didn't mean to be so overbearing, and maybe in her mind she was just being helpful. But . . . Elaine's idea of being helpful often did not jibe with anyone else's. She just couldn't help herself. The moment she perceived a vacuum she would rush right in. She's one of those people—and we all know them, in and out of show business—who just instantly suck all the oxygen out of the room. It was all Elaine, all the time. Me, me, me, me.

The benefit was a big success, and the audience had a great time, but I can't say that I did. The next day I told my manager, "I never, ever want to be inside a theater with her again, even for a benefit. If she's in the benefit, I'm not gonna do it. I don't want to have anything to do with her anymore."

I was upset and very, very angry. She was so talented, but it wasn't worth it. I had such admiration for her; she could go so deep into a lyric, that she could make it both personal and universal. I could learn from that, but the price was too high and life is too short. As time passed, I got over a lot of my anger, and in some ways I felt sorry for her.

One time when asked why she lived in hotels, she said, "Look, I don't have a lot of friends. So when I live in a hotel, I can have a conversation with the concierge and the elevator man." I think she was really sad. That was brought home to me when I was talking with Ralph Williams, who played the role of Arpad in *She Loves Me* and with whom I have kept in touch over the years. He and Elaine used to be very close, but a few years back he said to me, "I've had to give up Elaine. I can't do it anymore. It got to be too much."

Elaine had quite a reputation for being tight with a penny, always managing somehow to get free theater tickets—even wrangling free pantyhose when she was in a show. And she could definitely make short shrift of a buffet. If it was free, Elaine was on it. Because of her diabetes she carried a full slate of supplies with her at all times. We went to the theater together once—we saw *Art* in London—and she carried a big shopping bag filled with crackers, orange juice, and so forth. You name it and Elaine had it in that satchel. All through the play she was rummaging through her bag. She'd reach for some food, and then she'd rub her hands with her lotion. Next would be another sip of orange juice, then some cheese. We were escorted to the queen's waiting room, because if they think you're a big deal they treat you very nicely in London; they take your tickets and your coat, show you to your seat, and ask you what you would like to drink at the interval. And what did Elaine do in the queen's waiting room? Right there in front of the man helping us she gave herself an insulin shot.

Her behavior would get under my skin big time, and yet her work could be so damn great. For Sondheim's eightieth birthday concert with the New York Philharmonic, the show featured some incredibly talented women, chief among them Patti LuPone, Donna Murphy, and Bernadette Peters, but they gave Elaine the closing slot. Her rendition of "I'm Still Here" was brilliant. I thought it was sensational, and I e-mailed Steve Sondheim to tell him so.

In the end, I just decided to get over my frustration with her. She was never going to change, and I realized that so long as I didn't work with her, when I saw her it would be easy enough to be nice. In 2010 I substituted for her at a concert she had been scheduled to give; Elaine was replacing Angela Lansbury in *A Little Night Music* and couldn't fulfill the date, so I agreed to fill in for her. The evening was a success and also was the occasion of the most memorable opening patter I've ever had with an audience. After my opening number I looked out at the audience and said, "I know some of you may have expected to see Elaine Stritch. She is busy with *A Little Night Music*. But, you're not missing much. All she does is talk about all of the famous people she's fucked. I've fucked a lotta people, but they're not famous, so I don't talk about it!" The audience gasped—and then burst into wild laughter. I thought the building would explode! They may have expected that from Elaine, but definitely not from me.

Elaine would call me from time to time, and the surprising thing was that she would greet me as if we were bosom buddies. It was as if she assumed we were much closer than we really were. At the very end of her life she moved back to her native Michigan to live near her closest relatives. When she died, in July of 2014, her death was front-page news in the *New York Times*, which seemed only fitting. She'd have loved the placement. There will never be another like her. She could make me crazy, but a part of me loved her, too.

After the *Follies* concerts in 1985, I took on a full-scale musical in 1988, the infamous and ill-fated *Carrie*. The show was a Royal Shakespeare Company production based on the best-selling horror novel by Stephen King, and was to play in Stratford-Upon-Avon. From the start, everything went wrong, and the show became the stuff of legend for all of the wrong reasons.

This was offbeat material to begin with, a musical about a girl with telekinetic powers seeking revenge on those who have abused her. I was to play Margaret White, Carrie's fanatically religious mother who ultimately tries to kill her daughter to save the world from her destructive power. It was all a long way from Marian the Librarian. At the climax of the show there was going to be blood everywhere onstage as lives were ended or ruined—it was all pretty far out. And yet . . . I liked some of the score a great deal. Actually, there were two scores: one for Carrie and her mother, and the other, a 1950s rock-and-roll score, for the high school students. The relationship between mother and daughter had the potential to be complex and emotionally involving. The key word here is "potential"—because I think it didn't turn out that way.

Fran and Barry Weissler were originally slated to produce the show, and it was they who first asked me to sign on. I turned them down, but then director Terry Hands came to speak with me; Terry is a very smart, seductive man, and he explained certain scenes in such clear detail that I could see myself in them. I knew I could perform the show he described, and it was exciting to think of appearing in a Royal Shakespeare Company production. I said yes, but the one smart thing I did was sign only for England. There was no mention in my contract of my appearing in the transfer to Broadway. The company manager mentioned to me he was aware of my not being signed for New York and brought it up several times with the producer, who always said, "Later, I'm busy now."

In Terry's first meeting with Fran Weissler, she told him she wanted the show to have the feeling of *Grease*. He thought she meant "Greece" and the next time they met he had costume designs for the gym teacher and girls with all kinds of classical-era drapery. Fran and Barry dropped out, but by then Terry was wedded to the Grecian drapery and helmets. He was convinced that *Carrie* was a Greek tragedy. It's hard to believe this next point, but, please, believe me, it's true: sometime after *Carrie* Terry left the RSC, and was being interviewed about his career. When the subject of *Carrie* came up, he said: "I realize I made many mistakes with *Carrie*. Chiefly among them I thought the show was a Greek tragedy. I was wrong. It's a Roman tragedy."

Soon after we started rehearsals I realized that not one person involved had ever put together a new musical from scratch. The most basic, essential building blocks eluded the creators, and at one point during technical rehearsals the entire company and orchestra sat doing absolutely nothing while Terry Hands lit the show. Tens of thousands of dollars were flying out the window. I actually went to the lead producer, Friedrich Kurz, and told him, "These people don't know what they're doing. Put whatever deutschmarks you have left in your pocket and walk away. It will be a disaster." Friedrich didn't listen—he felt he had to honor his commitment.

I went to Terry and said, "There's nothing wrong with asking for help—everyone does it all the time." But no one was willing to acknowledge the need for help in nearly every department. They didn't even have a dance arranger lined up, and I asked for Wally Harper to come over to London and begin work on arrangements. The composer, Michael Gore, was furious when Wally arrived. He felt I just wanted Wally with us to join my camp, and I think he was afraid Wally might want to change some of his music. But the existing dance arrangements were far from the only problem. Debbie Allen, the choreographer, had also never put a new show together before. Since *Oklahoma!* back in 1943, musical numbers have had to further the story, but the numbers in *Carrie* came across like nice dances for television—nothing more. Matters were not helped when I gave an interview and, when asked how it was all progressing, blurted out: "We're doing a lot of work but it's like rearranging the deck chairs on the *Titanic*."

I began keeping a journal because the entire experience soon became utterly surreal. I said to the production stage manager that no one could believe what was happening, because they would have no frame of reference.

I knew from day one that I was not doing my best work because I never felt comfortable with the material. As rehearsals continued I told the creators that the mother—namely, me—needed a song about how horrible it would be to kill her daughter. Better yet, I said, give her a song during which she makes the decision to kill her and we see what her thoughts are. They agreed and then wrote a beautiful song about how quiet the house would be without Carrie. WRONG. It was a lovely song, but it didn't touch on what I had asked for. I think they didn't always know which parts of the story should be musicalized.

No one had thought through any of the practicalities. One of the early scenes took place in the doorless showers of the girls' high school locker room, so while they were in the shower the audience could clearly see their microphone battery packs and that they were wearing their underclothes. Believability went right out the window. When the same girls put on their Grecian clothes for gym class in present-day United States, you had to be thinking, "What the hell is going on?"

In the end, we had a show made up of two separate and distinct musicals: one was about the kids in Carrie's high school, and the other was a serious musical drama about Carrie (played by the terrific and very young Linzi Hateley) and her mother. The two shows never came together, and audiences were justifiably confused—and sometimes provoked into fits of unintended laughter.

I left the show at the end of the engagement in England, but I did go to see it during its very brief run on Broadway in May of 1988. It was still a disaster, and they hadn't solved any of the basic problems, let alone details like why the gym teacher was leading class in high-heeled pumps . . . I was incredibly relieved not to be a part of the show but found myself moved by Linzi, who at the very young age of seventeen gave a strong, solid performance. She had turned in a terrific professional performance in England and was even better in New York. There was so much chaos putting this show on, and she was the rock that held us all together, but she couldn't make this wrongheaded show into a hit. *Carrie* had been a very popular, successful book, and a very popular, successful movie. The musical proved to be neither. In 2012 it came back as a much smaller-scale musical. The reviews were far from vitriolic this time, most of them remarking on how bland the show now seemed, as if all the juice had been drained out of it. It ran for one month and then quietly disappeared.

In 1994, six years after *Carrie*, I returned to London to appear in concert at the Sadler's Wells Theatre. I had a great time, the show was recorded live, and I received perhaps the most laudatory review I've ever received, from Alastair Macaulay in the *Financial Times*: "Barbara Cook is the greatest singer in the world. . . . Ms. Cook is the only popular singer active today who should be taken seriously by lovers of classical music. Has any singer since Callas matched Cook's sense of musical architecture? I doubt it." I know we're not supposed to take reviews seriously—good or bad—but I ain't gonna forget that one. I was grateful for the praise, but I also maintained a healthy dose of self-doubt—was I really that good? I knew I was singing well, but I always feel there's more to learn. What I do think is true is that by this time I felt so free onstage that it was like entering a kind of zone, my own world, where sometimes, when the song ended, I didn't really want to come back, because it felt so good in there.

In the same year as the Sadler's Wells concerts I was inducted into the Theater Hall of Fame, in a ceremony at New York's Gershwin Theatre. It was a great honor, but I don't think of myself as being in a "hall of fame." I feel like I'm still a work in progress. (I felt the same way in 2002, when I was named a "living landmark" by the New York Landmarks Conservancy, for "having defined the city in my own legendary way." Those are very nice words, but obviously I can't begin to think of myself that way. A living landmark? I just want to keep working. And maybe learn to swear a little less.)

Wally and I continued with a busy schedule of concerts and recordings, including an appearance at the Sydney Opera House as part of the 2000 Summer Olympics Arts Festival. The biggest milestone, however was the show we called *Mostly Sondheim*, which premiered at Carnegie Hall in 2001 and was subsequently released as a live recording that sold very well.

Both the show itself and that inspired title were Wally's ideas. He's the one who remembered an article in the Sunday *New York Times Magazine* in which Stephen Sondheim listed a lot of songs he wishes he had written. Wally said "Let's do a show—half the songs will be by Stephen and half will be those he wishes he had written." We could call it *Mostly Sondheim*. It was a brilliant idea.

After Carnegie Hall we took the show to London's West End, to the Lyric Theatre, and I received two Olivier Award nominations, one for Best Entertainment and another for Best Actress in a Musical. I didn't win either award, but that was fine with me; I was performing material I loved, singing songs that were so complex and sophisticated that I discovered new facets at every single performance. After London we took the show to Lincoln Center, where we performed it from December 2001 until August 2002. I received a Tony nomination for Best Theatrical Event, and although I didn't win I was thrilled with the reception the show received. It wasn't just the chance to explore Stephen's gems like "In Buddy's Eyes" from *Follies*; it was also the sheer fun of singing songs none of us ever imagined Stephen might have wished he'd written, like "Waiting for the Robert E. Lee" and "Hard Hearted Hannah." Mike Nichols came to see the show and wrote me a lovely letter about how much he had enjoyed the evening: "You and Wally breathe together and it's impossible to know where one leaves off and the other begins. Together you are immortal. You gave us something we will never forget. I had Judy at Carnegie Hall, for which I was there, and now you at the Beaumont. Thank you." I was overwhelmed. Coming from Mike Nichols, that letter meant everything.

Wally and I then put together one more conceptual concert, *Barbara Cook's Broadway!*, which we performed in 2004 at Lincoln Center Theater. I received a New York Drama Critics' Circle Award and was nominated for a Drama Desk Award for Outstanding Solo Performance, but what I remember most clearly from the show is the extraordinary present Wally gave to me.

I talked in the show about always having wanted to see my name in lights—real electric lights, real old-fashioned bulbs—and it was Wally who made that happen. I was onstage at Lincoln Center, chatting with the audience, when they all started to applaud; I didn't know what was happening until I turned around and saw, descending from the flies, a sign composed of brightly lit bulbs that spelled out *Barbara Cook's Broadway!* I was thrilled, and at first I thought it was the theater that had come up with the sign. In fact, it was another of Wally's wonderfully generous gestures. He couldn't say "I love you" to me, but he expressed that love through the gift of that wonderful sign.

THROUGHOUT MY THIRTY years of working with Wally, alcohol abuse remained a severe problem in his life. There's no other way to say it: Wally was a major, major drunk from the moment I met him. He was what is called a high-functioning alcoholic. Very dangerous. He tried to fool himself into thinking otherwise. He thought, "So I drink. So what! I show up. I do the work. Leave me alone." I continued to drink throughout our first three years together. But in the very first weeks we worked as a team, he'd ask me if I wanted a drink. And when I asked him if *he* was going to have one, he'd say, "No—Max [his friend] and I have decided that if we don't drink for a month, then we're not alcoholics." It's a ridiculous statement. If you need to play that game, then, sorry, you *are* an alcoholic. If you don't have a problem with drinking, that game wouldn't even occur to you.

I said to him one day, "You know, I'll bet you became a drinker as soon as you left your family and went away to school." "Absolutely," he said. "I was seventeen." Which means that he drank alcoholically from age seventeen until it killed him at age sixty-three. He would not go to a doctor for help with his problem. He had bleeding hemorrhoids and refused to have a checkup, yet would somehow find a way to get doctors to give him drugs. He had a pharmaceutical book and he would look up what drugs were right for which condition, and he would treat himself.

His fear of doctors was pathological, and it went beyond not trusting them. He would make up lies about doctors, something I found out about in a strange way. Wally became very close friends with Peter Matz, the orchestrator and arranger famous for his work on the early Streisand albums. Wally and Peter were really close. They were like brothers, and when Peter died from cancer, Wally was devastated. He continued a close friendship with Peter's wife, Marilyn. At some point after Peter's death, Wally was telling several of us about how Peter had died, describing how the doctors had actually made his condition worse. When I happened to mention this to Marilyn—"I'm so sorry that the doctors did that"— she was totally mystified. "What? That never happened." Wally had invented it. It was just a flat-out lie.

Lying becomes a way of life for alcoholics, which I certainly know firsthand. When I was drinking, I would phone and say, "Oh I'm so sorry I can't come to the dinner party." This would be at the last minute, completely disrupting the hostess's plans. I just couldn't get it together because it was hard for me to function, and hard to be with people, so I lied in order to break the commitment.

I adored Wally, and, honestly, through all those years when we worked together I never felt I was the star of the show—he was. He always called the shots. I usually don't hand over control, but I had such great respect for him musically, as he did for me, that it was hardly ever a problem to do so. Which is not to say it was always smooth sailing.

In the recording studio, for example, he could be really mean. We were always under the gun in the studio because our recordings were made on a minimal budget. We didn't have time or money to waste, so it was always push, push, push. The problem was that if we were slipping behind schedule, Wally would sometimes excoriate me in front of the band. Here's what would happen. We'd have a first read-through of the orchestration. I would have notes based on what we just did, but Wally would often want to record the second time through, before I had a chance to voice my comments. As a result, sometimes I would stop during the second take to fix something, and then Wally would explode with anger. I think a lot of other singers, after being treated harshly in front of the orchestra, would have just said, "Shut the fuck up. I'm getting somebody else." I didn't, and couldn't, and we worked through it, but it was often unpleasant.

Wally did try a couple of times to stop drinking, but he was never really willing to give up control. He decided to detox himself at one point, a very dangerous thing to do. He convinced a close friend, a woman who was in love with him, to help him detox. He had had several seizures by this time and at the hospital he had been told he had a vitamin deficiency. I brought in a doctor friend of ours to see him, and the doctor gave him tranquilizers, not knowing that Wally would use them to detox. So, armed with vitamins and tranquilizers, Wally set out to detox himself. How he decided that this constituted a rational course of medical treatment I have no idea. I waited four or five days before I went over to his apartment; one of the reasons I needed to see him was to decide if he would be able to play a date we had coming up, and when he came out of his room I was horrified. He shuffled out of his room all bent over, and was so drugged he could hardly speak. I had to tell him I would have to find somebody else to play for me. "No, no. I can do it," he mumbled over and over.

The situation was made worse by the fact that his partner loved wine, and even though two doctors had said to get all the alcohol out of the house, Wally's partner kept the wine. I said to him, "Get this out of here," and he replied, "Wally doesn't drink wine, so it's okay." I was stupefied, because I knew—when you're desperate you'll drink anything.

Working with Wally the last few years of his life often became a nightmare. He just wouldn't or couldn't stop drinking. I told him a number of times his drinking was going to kill him. I believed that, but at the same time I don't think I could really imagine him dying.

Ultimately cirrhosis of the liver killed him, though what he really died from was hemorrhaging from his esophagus, which I understand is common with cirrhosis. I was so angry with him for not stopping the drinking, but I could never get through to him. His feeling was, in essence, "Look, I'm here, I'm doing the work, so leave me alone." The reality was that he couldn't always do the work properly. When it came time to record *Barbara Cook's Broadway!*, it was decided we'd record the show live at an evening performance at Lincoln Center. That afternoon, Wally came in for the sound check so drunk that he could barely find the piano, let alone play. I was thinking, "What the hell? We're going to record and you can't even walk straight?" He went home, took a nap, and when he came back he was somehow okay. He was still drunk, but the sort of drunk where he could play. I could never be entirely certain which version of Wally would show up. Toward the end of his life, things got so bad that several times I toyed with the idea of working with someone else, but I never took that step because Wally impaired was still better than most sober. *Barbara Cook's Broadway!* proved to be a big success and Wally was a big reason for that triumph.

One day I went to Wally's apartment to rehearse and he was simply too far gone to work. I said, "Okay, Wal, I'm going home now. I'll be back tomorrow. Please be ready to work." Several times I would have to go home, so when we *were* able to work, I felt I wanted to "reward" him, and in a lighthearted way, I would say, "Today you get a bluebird on your paper." Day by day, the bluebirds accumulated, and on opening night, Wally gave me a real blue parakeet. Wally's way of telling me he loved me.

When he was drinking, Wally could display a terrible temper, yet at the same time he was one of the most generous people I've ever known, particularly with his time. He was always ready to assist young talent in any way he could, helping the Tony Award–winning lyricist David Zippel (*City of Angels*) when he first came to New York from Harvard. And together we first heard Michael Kosarin playing in the lounge of a nightclub in North Carolina when he was still at Duke University. Michael has now been music supervisor, arranger, producer, and conductor for composer Alan Menken's theatrical, film, and television music worldwide since 1993, and it was Wally who paved the way for him in New York.

I've often thought that Wally was disappointed in himself—disappointed that he hadn't been able to compose a show for Broadway, because when he came to New York that had been his greatest ambition. He did some wonderful work on shows with Tommy Tune—*A Day in Hollywood, A Night in the Ukraine, My One and Only*—but those were never *his* shows. He had arranged but not composed. I think as much as Wally admired Stephen Sondheim, he was jealous of Stephen's extraordinary career. Back in the early 1980s, even before the *Follies* concerts, I had run into Stephen on the street, and he said "Barbara—why don't you ever sing my songs?" Needless to say, I was thrilled to hear Stephen say that, but Wally was, at first, very reluctant to include Sondheim songs in our repertoire. After the *Follies* concerts, Wally finally gave in, overcame his jealousy, and we placed Sondheim's music throughout our shows.

We celebrated Wally's sixty-third birthday in London while playing at the Haymarket Theatre. I could never have imagined that he would be dead just one month later. But as it turned out, we had only one more concert date together, in St. Louis. I wrote a journal entry at the time detailing just how troubled Wally was: the night of our performance in St. Louis his gums were bleeding. He had a big bump on his forehead and bruises on his face, all of which he explained by saying that he had walked into a door he thought was open. It's impossible to know what really happened, but I told him to come into my dressing room and I would try to cover the bruises with some of my makeup. He was spreading it on his forehead when I noticed there was blood there, too. I asked what was wrong. He said his thumb was bleeding. As always, he drank too much before going onstage, but was okay until the very end of the show when he goofed up and the sound man couldn't figure out what was going on. As a result, one of the climactic songs of the evening didn't land properly. I was angry and exasperated, a state of affairs that shifted to fear when, after the show, the wardrobe mistress came into my room and asked, "Is everybody all right?" I answered yes, at which point she told me that she'd noticed blood on the floor of Wally's room.

The next day we were flying back to New York, and when we were seated by the gate, waiting to board, Wally said he was going to get a Sunday *New York Times*. As he walked away I noticed a very large dark-red stain the size of a dinner plate on the seat of the raincoat he was wearing. I was embarrassed for him, and when I finally mentioned it to him, he said that it had happened the night before at our hotel. He was visiting with a friend who he said spilled remoulade sauce on one of the chairs. He then sat down, thinking he'd convinced me, but I knew that wasn't true. The cirrhosis had caused him to hemorrhage. That was on a Sunday. The next Wednesday he and his partner Alan Gruet went out to dinner separately. Wally had returned before Alan, who, when he came back, saw Wally lying on the floor of the living room. He wasn't immediately alarmed because it wasn't the first time he had found him like that, but then he saw Wally was bleeding badly. Even then Wally resisted medical attention, but Alan got him to Roosevelt Hospital, where they tried to stop the bleeding. It didn't work, and on the morning of October 8, 2004, exactly one month after his sixty-third birthday, Wally died.

Because he had died early in the morning there was time to let people know and to organize a gathering at my apartment where we could all grieve and reminisce. The night of his death, I confess, I felt mostly anger and frustration. Now, eleven years later, I'm feeling so much love for him, and I'm drowning in sorrow.

It had been clear to all of us for a long time both that his life was out of control and that he was dreadfully ill, but I somehow felt this wasn't supposed to happen to him. Not to Wally Harper. So many people depended on him for so much, beginning with his incredible musical knowledge; he actually was a great musical leader and made you feel that he had all the answers. He imparted a great sense of security.

I like to remember Wally in terms of his overwhelming talent. His phrasing while playing could be nothing short of achingly beautiful. One conductor called Wally "a musician's musician, a genius even—he made the piano sing." I thought that was a great way to put it, because while the fact that Wally always felt the rules did not apply to him caused problems in his personal life, it also gave him free rein when putting together those glorious arrangements.

I loved so much about Wally, particularly his incredible sense of humor. Years back, he had found us a tax man who was a real character; this man saved us thousands upon thousands of dollars but I never fully understood how he did it. I didn't want to know. He also got us in trouble from time to time. Wally's name for him? J. P. Loophole.

The witticisms would just pour out of him, both verbally and musically. When he was a fourteen-year-old boy in Ohio playing organ for Sunday church services, he was asked to provide music while the ushers returned to the altar with the day's offering. Wally's choice of music? A Bach-tinged arrangement of "We're in the Money."

(Not surprisingly, the pastor told Wally there would be no repeat performance of *that* number . . .)

Toward the end of his life he worked on several shows with Sherman Yellen, who had written the books for the musicals *The Rothschilds* and *Rex*. Somehow Sherman and Wally got the idea that Sherman could write lyrics to Wally's music, but on the first day they began working together, Sherman was very nervous and said, "Wal, I'm not so sure this is a good idea. You know, I've never written lyrics before, and I'm feeling pretty apprehensive about it." To which Wally retorted, "Are you kidding? A Jew and a homosexual—we can't miss."

"But, Wal, I have to tell you I'm not much of a Jew."

"That's okay," replied Wally, "because I'm one hell of a homosexual!"

Although Wally could never solve his problem with alcohol, I think he was genuinely happy for me when I stopped drinking.

He said to his then partner, Michael: "Of all the people I know, Barbara has changed her life for the better more than anybody I've ever known." He saw how I had pulled myself together, finally owned an apartment I loved, and that I took great pride in my work. He had seen me in the darkest of times, and he was so happy for me. What an extraordinary generosity of spirit he possessed.

Just after Wally died, Audra McDonald told me that she had a dream about him. She was visiting him in heaven and he said, "I almost didn't get in here, you know." "Why?" she asked, and he showed her his liver. "So how did you get in?" she persisted. And he showed her his heart.

For all the glamorous success and excess of his life, he was in some ways still the little boy from Akron, Ohio. When in 2003 we were invited to perform in the party scene of the Metropolitan Opera's annual New Year's Eve production of *The Merry Widow*, Wally was enlisted to conduct the orchestra. When he got up for the first rehearsal it just overwhelmed him—and he started to cry.

I miss him very much.

I WAS HAVING a great time giving concerts all over the world, and Jerry Kravat kept it all the more interesting by constantly thinking up new opportunities for me. Jerry wasn't just a manager—he was Jerry Kravat Entertainment Services and had his fingers in lots of pies and his toes in lots of rivers. He was a workaholic and really went all out on my behalf. He was constantly on the phone drumming up work for me and always thinking in terms of "What's the next big event we can do for you?"

He was responsible for my playing the Metropolitan Opera House in January 2006, an event he worked on for several years. Along with Yves Montand and Vladimir Horowitz, I became one of only three solo artists who have been presented by the Met itself as part of their regular season.

Most of the time when I'm performing I have my nerves pretty much under control, but occasionally, before a big concert, when I'm standing in the wings, waiting to walk out, I can frankly be scared. That's no good, and the Metropolitan Opera concert was definitely one of those occasions. But—I've developed a way to help myself through times like that. The first thing I do is plant my feet firmly on the floor and imagine I'm getting power flowing into my body from the depths of the earth. Then I think of how fortunate I am to have the gift of being able to sing. I tell myself to go out and give it back. Give the gift back. That gets me out of the realm of ego, and then I don't worry about what people will think about my singing or what they might think about my appearance. I'm calmer. After a couple of songs, I'm comfortable and having fun.

I was more than a little nervous to be singing at the Metropolitan Opera House, but while waiting to go on I wasn't so nervous that I failed to notice how worn the curtain appeared from the back. I thought about the number of times it had been held for great artists like Luciano Pavarotti, Marilyn Horne, Renée Fleming, Placido Domingo, and the amazing Leontyne Price. WOW! I had such respect for those giants.

When I walked onstage that night at the Met, the entire audience stood up, applauding. It was an extraordinary moment. I had never dared dream about appearing at the Metropolitan Opera House. Me? Barbara Cook, little nine-year-old Barbara Cook deserting her playmates to go inside to listen to the Met's Saturday-afternoon broadcasts? I had terrific guest artists that night: Josh Groban, Elaine Stritch, Audra McDonald. It was, in short, a thrilling night for me.

It was also Jerry's idea to celebrate my eightieth birthday, in 2007, with New York Philharmonic concerts at Avery Fisher Hall. Here I was, back at Avery Fisher twenty-two years after the *Follies* concerts, and I had a ball. Singing again with the Philharmonic—I think anyone would be hard-pressed to come up with a better way to celebrate an eightieth birthday.

Sadly, one year after the birthday concerts Jerry died. We had worked together for twenty-nine great years and we had a terrific journey together. How I miss him. He was my manager, but more than that, he was my friend.

Although *Mostly Sondheim* and *Barbara Cook's Broadway!* were successes, they were one-woman concerts, just as were the nights at the Metropolitan Opera and Avery Fisher Hall. I still had not returned to Broadway in a musical since 1971's *The Grass Harp*, a situation that changed in 2010 when I appeared in the Roundabout Theatre's production of *Sondheim on Sondheim*, a compilation of Stephen's work sung by a cast of eight.

This was not a traditional book musical, but rather an overview of Stephen's amazing career in the theater. Filmed interviews with Stephen supplied the narrative flow and served to introduce the various numbers. Material doesn't get any better than these extraordinary songs, and when James Lapine asked me to appear in the show, I said yes immediately.

Still, I was nervous before we started. Not only was this my first Broadway musical in over thirty years, but it was not exactly going to be low profile. I was also eighty-two years old, and worried about having the stamina to do eight shows a week. There was concern about remembering all the words because I sometimes forget a few lyrics when I do my shows and concerts. When that happens, I fix it and carry on, but I felt I couldn't do that in this show. I talked to James about it and he kindly arranged a monitor for me. I remember glancing at it a couple of times, but just knowing it was there took a great load off my shoulders.

We had a great cast including Vanessa Williams, Norm Lewis, and Tom Wopat, and while I was nervous, I was also eager. Stephen was not in the rehearsal room each day, leaving the direction to James Lapine, but he came to a later run-through, along with Frank Rich. He gave us very specific notes after our run-through: how he preferred us to pronounce certain words, when to guard against "scooping" notes. A lot of people think of Stephen as tough and intellectual, and that his work reflects a certain edginess. I think one reason why I relate to his work so well is that I enjoy bringing out the warm and human side of his work. He is, in fact, a very caring, emotional person. He is exacting about his work, but he is also a very appreciative audience, and a very emotional one as well. When moved, he cries easily.

Surprisingly, I didn't have any trouble reentering the world of performing eight shows a week. We opened in April of 2010 and ran for our scheduled three months; I was thrilled to receive a Tony nomination, along with my fellow octogenarian Angela Lansbury, who was appearing in *A Little Night Music*. Much as I would have liked to win, I knew that Katie Finneran was going to take home the prize for her hilarious performance in *Promises, Promises*. But, fifty-plus years after I had won the Tony for *Music Man* I had received another nomination and was very happy about that fact.

And then, miracle of miracles: the Kennedy Center Honors.

When I received the honor in December of 2011 I was overwhelmed. Never, never, never did I think that would happen for me. There are so many who have deserved the honor and never received it. Maybe they died too soon, which matters because you have to show up to receive it. In essence, it's a lifetime achievement award, and I was so pleased to be in that group of five honorees which included Meryl Streep, Yo-Yo Ma, Neil Diamond, and the great saxophonist Sonny Rollins.

Some people may think I don't belong on that list. The truth is that much of the time I wonder about it myself. I know I'm good. But am I Jimmy Cagney good? Am I Gregory Peck good? Am I Fred Astaire good?

On the night the awards ceremony was shown on television I was working and couldn't watch the telecast. When I came offstage my assistant, Louise, yelled, "You're trending! You're trending!" I had no idea what the hell she was talking about. She might as well have been speaking Swahili, but she was actually talking about Twitter. Evidently I was one of the top-ten subjects being tweeted about worldwide. Somebody sent me those tweets and I looked through many of them, scrolling through dozens and dozens of lovely messages. My favorite tweet, of course, was: "Who the fuck is Barbara Cook?" I liked that one because part of me was thinking, "Who the fuck thinks Barbara Cook deserves to be a part of this amazing group of people?"

The Kennedy Center Honors were the icing on the cake for me; just to be mentioned in the same breath as those incredible artists was a gift. I had been hearing rumors that I might receive the award—hints from Michael Kaiser and Adrienne Arsht—but if there is anything I've learned from sixty-plus years in the business, it's that talk is cheap and nothing's real until it happens. For at least a dozen years Jerry Kravat and a Washington-based friend, Lester Hyman, had been lobbying on my behalf, which is not at all an unusual thing for people to do. Typically, supporters begin writing letters, contacting other people, suggesting that their favorite be honored.

Even as Jerry began this campaign for me all those years ago, he didn't believe it would actually happen. He said, "I don't think there's a chance in hell that this will come through, but let's go through the motions and see how it turns out." And I thought to myself, "If this should happen it will make everything okay. It will make those years when I was unemployable, when I couldn't stop drinking, when I should have been doing my best work in the theater, okay. It will make it all okay." So when I heard I was on the short list, I was excited but tried not to get my hopes up too high or think about it too much. Adrienne and Michael had both been telling me for a long time that things looked good for me, and they said it so often that I finally said to Adrienne: "Listen, I need to tell you that after all you and Michael have said, if this doesn't happen I'm going to have to kill both of you!"

It's embarrassing now to think about how much I wanted the honor. I didn't believe it would happen. I wonder if anyone does. You're officially informed of the honor by letter, and the funniest part was that even after the public announcement had been made and I had received the letter asking me to accept the honor, I still had trouble believing it. (Steven Spielberg said that he had to have his assistant read it to him twice before he believed it.)

The honors encompass a weekend of events in Washington, D.C.—the first weekend in December. It's all surprisingly low-key. On Saturday night they have a dinner at the State Department, where they come up behind you and put the medal around your neck while the secretary of state talks about you and your career. The placing of the medal may be low-key, but make no mistake, it is still a big deal.

So too is the ceremony itself at the Kennedy Center, on Sunday. Along with your four fellow honorees, you sit in a special box with the president and first lady while others pay tribute to your career. You don't have to work, but in effect you end up taking the best curtain call imaginable! Adam was with me as my escort, and I just wish Jerry Kravat and Wally Harper could have been there as well. They had both died a few years before this happened, and I sure thought about them that night. Patti LuPone, Audra McDonald, Sutton Foster, and others paid tribute to me from the stage and it was overwhelming. When all was said and done, the strongest feeling I held inside was one of being understood. Somebody "got it." A lot of people "got it." As an artist I couldn't have asked for more.

BROADWAY TODAY IS a far different place than it was in the late 1950s and early sixties. Perhaps the biggest difference lies in the way careers now develop. In those days you didn't suddenly go from featured player to headliner. You had to earn it. That tradition of really earning your name above the title has vanished. The stakes are so high now that producers want to import a well-known Hollywood name, even for a limited run, in order to pack the theater, turn a profit, and make a quick getaway. Some theater stars do exist, of course—Sutton Foster, Kelli O'Hara, and Audra McDonald come to mind—but half a century ago, shows would have been written for them. These talented women now perform in concerts not just because they want to, but also because they have to. It used to be that you didn't do concerts and cabaret on the side—you just landed another show. Now it could be years between musicals, even for the biggest names on Broadway.

They tell me now that I was part of Broadway's Golden Age, the era that really seemed to start with *Oklahoma!* in 1943. I know that *Show Boat* in 1927 changed the playing field, but with *Oklahoma!* the entire landscape of musical theater changed. You could no longer get away with the unadulterated silliness that was nothing more than an excuse for songs, and, following the lead of Oscar Hammerstein II, creators now utilized an integrated approach, combining dialogue, music, lyrics, and dance in order to tell a meaningful story. Well, my first show was *Flahooley*, in 1951, and the truth is I didn't know I was part of any golden age. I wish somebody had told me. I would have had a lot more fun.

Sometimes I ask an audience, "Do you think we're in a golden age now?" I hear a lot of moans coming back at me. Well, we could be. I think what we have to do is enjoy every day just as much as we can because thirty years from now you could wake up and they'll tell you that you were in a golden age, and you'd feel like a fool if you didn't.

For a long time I wasn't fully aware of how much of my own life I put into interpreting lyrics, into communicating on a very personal level with the audience. But when I was accepting the Sondheim award from City Opera, in my acceptance speech I said: "I thank you so much for this. I think by giving me this award you not only honor my work, but you also honor my life, because that's what I do—I put my life, everything that ever happened to me, the good and the bad, into these songs." I believe art that is authentic can be healing. I suppose that I've come to think of myself as a salesman, because I really do believe that what I have to say through my songs can help people.

Putting your life into your art—this is what I try to teach students in the master classes I conduct at venues like the Boston Conservatory of Music, and at Juilliard. "Stop worrying about how you look and how you sound. Concentrate on what you are trying to say with this song." The words have to matter: Who is the character? What are they really singing about? Are they singing one thing but meaning another? Oftentimes students come in and they just want you to know right away that they can SING, in capital letters. They come on like singing machines. Then—slowly,

slowly, slowly, I get them to be human beings again. It almost always works. It's quite exciting and very moving.

If I had to put it into one sentence, the most important lesson I want to instill in singers is: "You are enough."

I tell my students: "Work toward embracing yourself and who you are. You don't need to look like anybody else. You don't need to sound like anybody else. Have the courage to give us your true self.

"You are enough.

"You are always enough.

"We are always enough."

When any of us sings what has come to be known as the Great American Songbook, it's not about showing off vocally à la *American Idol*. You want the song to sound conversational. We're Americans—sing like you talk. That's what Sinatra was so great at—that sense of conversational intimacy with the listener.

When I teach master classes, I often think of a wonderful piece of advice from my ex-husband. Shortly before David died, Adam went to visit him in Los Angeles. Adam asked him, "Dad, can you tell me what you think is the most important thing you learned from Lee Strasberg?" He thought for a moment and then simply said, "Be there." That said it all as far as I'm concerned. That's what I impress upon the students. We need to "be there" as performers, but also need to "be there" in life. It's not always easy to do, but it is infinitely rewarding.

We all change as we age. I sure as hell hope I am not the same person I was fifty years ago. Change really is the only constant in life, and acceptance of that change can be rough, but essential.

In the interesting way that today's complicated family life sometimes unfolds, I finally saw my ex-husband after twenty-five years when Adam and I went to Italy for the wedding of his brother Jacob—David's son with his second wife, Beth. Adam and I flew to Rome, and when we were shopping for china in Portofino right before the wedding, Adam happened to glance toward the door and then whispered to me, "Mom, David LeGrant just walked in." Adam had not seen his father in eighteen years, but our joint re-union was pleasant—no bickering, no recriminations, just mother, father, and son together again for a brief moment.

Adam had not seen David for so many years because David had proved to be just as difficult toward Adam as he was with me; when Adam was growing up, he would tease him about not being athletic, in effect deriding him for not turning out exactly as David wanted and envisioned. Now, as adults, we could speak calmly, genuinely glad to see each other. We had all changed. I was so very happy about this turn of events: I had wanted David back in Adam's life, and now he was.

When Adam turned fifty, in 2009, I gave him a big birthday party, and David returned to New York for the first time since 1978. The good feelings engendered by our meeting in Italy remained, and as long as we stayed away from certain subjects we could have talked twenty-four hours a day. David remained difficult, but we all are in our own ways, and I was very grateful that he had played such a huge part in my life.

When David died, in July of 2011, I was surprised that it hurt so much. We had been divorced for forty-six years, and while I've never once doubted that the divorce was the right thing to do, whatever animosity I once held toward him had long since faded. I felt so bad when he died, and I think it's because his death brought back the memories of our life together, sending me back to that time and place when we were so young, in love, and with all of our adult lives ahead of us. I loved David. He was the father of my beloved son, and for those reasons I felt his loss with a depth of feeling that surprised me. Memories can be wonderful, but they can also wound.

At the time of David's death I had one of those two a.m. soul talks with a close friend. We were pondering whether either one of us had ever truly been in love. I think that very few people experience real love, by which I mean honest-to-God you-want-to-put-the-other-person's-needs-before-your-own kind of love. It sure doesn't happen often. I was in a deep first love with Herb Shriner that contained a certain degree of madness, because I was obsessed with him. But did I love him? Infatuation is totally different from love. David? I cared about him certainly and I was obviously attracted to him. But—did I love him to the depths of my soul? I'm still not sure. Arthur? I don't know. I just don't know.

As you get older, you realize more fully just how mysterious life can be—wonderful and puzzling, damaging and life-affirming. You may not have the physical gifts you possessed as a youngster, but you can draw on all of your experiences in an attempt to understand what it all means and to continue going on. I think back to a long-ago afternoon rehearsal at Avery Fisher Hall. I was sitting in the front row with Arthur Schwartz as the fellow onstage was singing "Dancing in the Dark," the masterpiece Arthur wrote with Howard Dietz.

I said, "God, Arthur, it must feel so good to have written such a gorgeous melody." And he said, "Yes, but you know, very few people know what the song is about." Now, I have to admit, the music is so compelling that I, like so many others, thought it was a lovely song about dancing.

But—the song, as Arthur explained to me, is about life and death. The transience of life. The aching beauty we can never quite hold on to.

Howard Dietz wrote:

> *Dancing in the dark till the tune ends.*
> *We're dancing in the dark and it soon ends.*
> *We're waltzing in the wonder of why we're here.*
> *Time hurries by. We're here and gone.*
> *Looking for the light of a new love*
> *To brighten up the night. I have you, love.*
> *And we can face the music together*
> *Dancing in the dark.*

Wally and I performed that amazing song at our first Carnegie Hall concert in 1975, but I'd sing it differently now. This song, like all great art, speaks to us in different ways at different stages of our lives, precisely because we all keep changing. We become older and acquire a different understanding of the dark. Same thing with the Rodgers and Hart song "I Didn't Know What Time It Was." I recorded that in the 1950s for an all Rodgers and Hart album of ballads, and while my voice was fine, I can sing it now with so much more feeling and drama, for one reason:

I've lived.

I'M EIGHTY-EIGHT YEARS old and realize that I have arrived at the fourth stage of womanhood:

Childhood

Adolescence

Maturity

and . . . "You look wonderful!"

And, wonderful or not, I still believe I'm a work in progress. I'm still learning, still excited, still frustrated, but most of all still in the game. I don't make a point of memorizing reviews, good or bad because what matters is to keep growing, but Stephen Holden in the *New York Times* reviewed me fairly recently in terms that really resonated with me: "In whatever she sings, you sense a lifetime's experience being addressed from a perspective that is still capable of wonder. . . ." It's true. Perhaps when we get older we reexperience the sense of wonder we felt as youngsters, only now it's mixed in with a sense of gratitude. Note how the light hits the leaves on the tree. Look at the everyday beauty surrounding us . . .

I try to be fully present when I sing. If I'm fully engaged, there is a chance that my soul, for lack of a better word, can touch the souls of other people, and then there can be healing. We are, finally, so alone in this world, but sometimes, if only for a few moments, there can be a whole group of people blending with one another. No matter what the medium, through authentic art can come healing.

I don't sing the way I used to. In some ways, I sing better. Better than I did five years ago, and I believe I'll sing even better five years from now (that is if I'm still around; I sometimes forget how old I am). I don't have the range I used to have, and my voice has surely gotten darker, but I have more and more courage to move deeper and deeper into the lyrics. I don't sing "Glitter and Be Gay" anymore, but I can pack a lifetime's worth of beauty and joy and pain into a lyric in a way I never could have fifty years ago.

In twelve-step programs you are taught "You will learn not to regret the past." Well, I do regret the past, lots of it. I regret not being active in the theater when I was in my prime. It's painful to think of all those missed opportunities. But Adam, who is very wise in so many ways—certainly wiser than I am—sees the big picture in a way that I don't, and said something helpful to me on that very topic: "Mom, this is your journey. And where you are is pretty great. Look at you. Still singing. Still working. Respected in the business. Still with a thriving career. A lot of those people who were active when you wanted to be don't work anymore, or they are no longer with us. So—this is your journey." And that really helped me. Wally used to tell me: "We'll keep going until you drop onstage—with your walker!"

I can still feel a bit of a twinge of jealousy when I see or hear about someone getting a great career opportunity that I wish I had. "Oh damn. Why didn't I get that?" But it's only a twinge. I used to play a game with myself about career opportunities that centered on: "How would I feel about this if Florence Henderson got it?" Back in 1955, my face was on a giant billboard overlooking Broadway for *Plain and Fancy*. That billboard was huge! It was very impressive. The problem was that I just couldn't take it in. The best I could do was to think, "Well, if Florence Henderson was on the billboard I'd be impressed, so maybe the fact that I'm up there means something." I liked Florence a lot. We had formed a fast friendship while touring a whole season together in *Oklahoma!* but I was making her the gauge for my own career. That thought process is completely foreign to me now. I can put aside thoughts of jealousy and immediately say to myself, "You know—that belongs to them. It's okay. This belongs to me. It's all okay."

And it really is.

Sometimes life is so hard. But it's the only game in town, and we sure as hell didn't make the rules—so either we give up, which some people do, or we play along the best we can, and along the way there is glory, too.

I've been able to grasp bits of that glory all along the way.

I remain, most of all, grateful.